Praise for *Leve.*

"This book is a must-read for anyone looking to deepen their understanding of psychology-based coaching. It clearly distinguishes this approach from traditional practices, offering valuable insights into self-awareness, psychological flexibility, and the art of influence. Dr. Lampasso skillfully demystifies Acceptance and Commitment Therapy (ACT), making psychological flexibility skills understandable for the everyday reader. Offering the strategies that help break free from limiting beliefs, this book is essential for those eager to align their passion with purpose and elevate their impact."

—Kulliki Keller, ACT Therapist

"*Level Up Your Influence* by Sunni Lampasso, PsyD, is a powerful guide to self-awareness and influence that combines psychological insights with practical tools for personal and professional growth. The book's 4-Square Model helps readers identify and overcome internal obstacles, while exercises like "Catch, Label, and Pack" make the strategies immediately applicable. Lampasso's focus on psychological flexibility, through Acceptance and Commitment Training (ACT), offers a transformative approach to overcoming fear and anxiety, fostering resilience and adaptability. Filled with personal stories and real-life examples, the book encourages ethical and values-driven leadership, making it a valuable resource for anyone looking to lead with authenticity and purpose."

—Lloyd Erlemann, CEO, Kairos Executive Programs

"Dr. Sunni Lampasso has the professional training, experience, and insight to recognize the unique challenge we each face when we want to increase our personal and career impact. She offers ways to recognize self-limiting beliefs and change the narrative that may be keeping you from achieving your aspirations. This isn't psychological self-help or pixie dust that tells you everything will be OK, but rather a path to do the work we each need to do if we want to level up from where we find ourselves today. If there is a voice inside of you that says you should be achieving more than you are today, then this book is for you."

—**Marc Sokol,** PhD, organizational psychologist; fellow, American Psychological Association; president, Society of Consulting Psychology

"A career in any business, especially the music business, is a challenge. Dr. Sunni Lampasso's *Level Up Your Influence* is an entertaining and insightful look into understanding the importance of self-awareness for personal and professional growth. As a DJ with 20-plus years of experience, I found some practical strategies and real-life examples that I can put into practice to maximize growth. Her emphasis on self-care, seeking support, and staying connected to one's purpose is crucial for maintaining mental well-being in the highly competitive music industry. You can feel her passion for our livelihood, and I'm looking forward to sharing this book with my friends in the music industry."

—**Shawn 'DJSPAWN' Foley,** Billboard Dance Chart & Mixshow DJ

"In her compelling book, Level Up Your Influence, Dr. Sunni Lampasso provides an empowering roadmap clarifying how our repeated thoughts, feelings, and behaviors can either help us thrive or derail us from our purpose and goals. As a coaching psychologist, she provides practical strategies and an easy-to-use, invaluable 4-step model based on human behavior science that helps you identify your unique inner obstacles, get unstuck, and take courageous action toward your dreams. Highly recommend."

—**Dana Gionta,** PhD, founder & CEO, Dana Gionta Coaching LLC

"Many people call themselves a 'life coach' or 'executive coach' even though they have little to no qualifications. Dr. Lampasso stands out from this crowd as she is supremely qualified with a doctorate in psychology. Her book opened my eyes to the negative thought/feeling patterns we all have, and presented a precise road map to navigate a healthier path forward. This is the book I didn't know I needed."

—**Noel Thayer,** audiologist

"*Level Up Your Influence: A Self-Awareness Guide to Maximizing Your Growth and Unlocking Your Inner Leader* is an essential read for anyone striving to become a more effective leader and a better human. The book provides a clear and practical roadmap for personal and professional growth. Sunni weaves deeply personal tales of her own journey with anecdotes pulled right from her experience as a clinical psychologist, executive coach, and entrepreneur to guide the reader through their own journey into how they show up in the world and how they can lead and inspire others. Sunni provides a guide to leading a values-driven life, setting goals that will inspire us to persevere, and creating the muscle memory for identifying internal obstacles and our own thoughts and feelings that often block our progress. Whether you're a seasoned leader or someone beginning your journey of self-discovery, this book will empower you to unlock your potential and create a lasting impact. A must-read for those committed to becoming their best self!"

—**Heidi Davidson,** co-founder and CEO, Galvanize Worldwide

LEVEL UP YOUR INFLUENCE

SUNNI LAMPASSO, PsyD

LEVEL UP YOUR INFLUENCE

A Self-Awareness Guide to
**Maximizing Your Growth and
Unlocking Your Inner Leader**

First edition 2025

Copyright © Sunni Lampasso, PsyD 2025

All rights reserved. No part of this book may be reproduced, distributed, or transmitted in any form or by any means, including photocopying, recording, or other electronic or mechanical methods, without the prior written permission of the author, except for the use of quotations in a book review. For permission requests: sunni@shapingsuccessconsulting.com

Although every precaution has been taken to verify the accuracy of the information contained herein, the author assumes no responsibility for any errors or omissions. No liability is assumed for losses or damages that may result from the use of information contained within. You are responsible for your own choices, actions, and results.

ISBN: 979-8-9915164-0-2 (paperback)
ISBN: 979-8-9915164-1-9 (ebook)

Cover art by Marla Beth Enowitz
Cover and layout design by G Sharp Design, LLC

Email: Sunni@shapingsuccessconsulting.com
Instagram: @shaping_success
LinkedIn: https://www.linkedin.com/in/sunnilampasso/
Website: https://www.shapingsuccessconsulting.com/

To my dad: your enduring inspiration guides me
to help others unlock their potential, just as you
did for me and countless others.

TABLE OF CONTENTS

A Word from the Author 1

Part I

Chapter 1   Level Up Your Influence 5

Chapter 2   Psychology-Based Coaching 21

Part II

Chapter 3   Square #1: Identifying Internal Obstacles: Unhelpful Thoughts and Feelings 49

Chapter 4   Square #2: What Happens When Internal Obstacles Get in the Way? 83

Chapter 5   Square #3: Values and Purpose 107

Chapter 6   Square #4: Values-Based, Goal-Directed Action 127

Chapter 7   Influence, Leveled Up 143

Acknowledgments 163

About the Author 167

A WORD FROM THE AUTHOR

In today's world, the *influence* we have on others matters. Whether online or in the real world, we are all more aware of the influence we have (or lack).

The term "leader" is going out of style. Fewer of us identify with the business world's traditional view of a leader—historically a C-suite level professional working in a corporate environment.

Taking inspiration from social media, the term "*influencer*" might be a better way to describe today's next generation of leaders.

After all, influencers can describe everyone we are listening to and learning from. And, taking it a step further, whatever industry you are in, leveling up your influence is the key to growth.

PART I

Chapter 1: Level Up Your Influence

Chapter 2: Psychology-Based Coaching

CHAPTER 1

LEVEL UP YOUR INFLUENCE

> *"The greatest power one possesses*
> *is the power of influence."*
> **JOHN C. MAXWELL**

"You're never going to work again. You need to get on a housing list and file for long-term disability."

These words from a doctor hit me like a freight train, followed by a gut reaction of resistance. My internal response was loud: "Absolutely not! I'm going to figure out another way!"

But a part of me wondered—*would I never really work again?*

No—there had to be another way. I wasn't going to let anyone tell me that it was the end of a career I worked so hard for.

Instead, looking back, this was my first day on an entirely new path.

At that moment, sitting in my hospital gown in the doctor's office, I knew I had to help *myself*.

> **At that moment, sitting in my hospital gown in the doctor's office, I knew I had to help *myself*.**

It all started in 2004. I had just graduated from Alliant International University after completing my graduate course work in clinical psychology and multiple internships in a variety of different settings. On top of the thrill of graduating, I landed my first job as a Clinical Supervisor. Life was good: I had achieved my goal to earn a role that would help others. Finally, I could do the psychology work I felt called to do.

But that first year didn't go as planned.

Hired into a leadership position because of my degree and knowledge of psychology, I had limited practical experience with leadership. I found myself in a situation where:

- → I didn't know my job
- → I didn't know my team member's jobs, and
- → I didn't understand the essential skills required for effective leadership.

If I had any questions, I could ask someone, but it felt overwhelming. *What questions should I ask when I don't know anything?*

I was a well-meaning but clueless leader. I wanted to help the clients, but I had no idea how to support my team and develop their skills. And, worse, I didn't know how to support myself or develop my own skills.

My stress level was through the roof. Fear was an overwhelming emotion. I desperately wanted to do a good job but anxiety and imposter syndrome were growing. I didn't know what my strengths or areas for development were. This wasn't even a thought in my mind.

I began to feel like I wasn't good at this job. I had no strengths. I didn't feel heard when I asked for help, probably because I didn't know what help I needed. I began working harder as thoughts and feelings got in the way of observing wins. I didn't see any wins. My self-care began to decrease—I was too tired to go to the gym and I was up late at night worrying about what wasn't going well. Work was taking over my life and I thought about it way beyond work hours. The grind continued and I felt more defeated as each day passed.

Then—something wasn't right. One day, after a year of trying to manage so many spinning plates, my body completely shut down.

It began with severe migraines. Then I developed a virus that doctors couldn't figure out. They treated my symptoms and sent me to specialists, but after several weeks, the virus had resolved but the symptoms had not. The doctor visits continued. Instead of being consumed with work and the clients I served, I became consumed with doctor's appointments, diagnostic tests, and medications.

Cancer? Multiple sclerosis? These and other diseases were discussed at each specialist appointment. While the virus was never identified, cancer and MS were ruled out. Meanwhile, the virus caused havoc throughout my body, resulting in a series of diagnoses from various specialists. A different type of fear became the overarching theme of my life; health anxiety. Would I ever recover? Would I be able to work again?

The contrast between the two years was extreme: year one in a leadership role struggling to keep afloat, year two unable to work and collecting a series of health diagnoses. What I didn't know at the time was that these hardships would be the experiences that enabled me to discover the guidance of self-awareness, maximize my growth, and unlock my inner leader.

The shift from being stuck in a fear-based mindset came suddenly when I heard those words from the doctor that I would never work again. I knew I had to change everything I was doing, and I became determined to do it. And these changes needed to be in my thinking and what I was doing.

I needed to change:

- → My *work environment.* I wasn't set up for success and was suffering.
- → My *home environment.* I was a New Yorker who felt like I'd been on a 10-year vacation and was homesick.

I decided to move from Orange County, California back to my friends, the culture, the pace, and the seasons.

➔ My *health*. As a psychologist I knew how important it was to manage stress, and my therapist helped me with a barrage of my fearful thoughts about what my future might be like. My self-care had decreased to nothing, so I needed to get back on track if I was going to have a life beyond doctor's appointments and illness.

Wellness became my new focus, and I started implementing mindfulness techniques and exercising. Motivated by my two goals – move back home and get back to working – I prioritized self-care and self-awareness.

Never work again? Not quite.

Fast-forward to today. As I write this in 2024, I'm an executive coach and consultant helping leaders in organizations and business owners develop their leadership skillset and leverage their strengths using research-based tools. In addition, I combined my passion and purpose and carved out a coaching niche in the Electronic Dance Music (EDM) community.

I'm thankful for my journey, because along the way, I discovered the one big thing that was getting in the way of my work, life, and health. It was me – I was my biggest obstacle. It wasn't my job, it was what I didn't see about myself and my environment—it was me.

1. I couldn't lead or influence others because I was overwhelmed by unhelpful thoughts and feelings related

to fear and self-doubt. These inner obstacles caused me to avoid searching for solutions to change my work situation. I felt stuck.

2. I lost sight of something that was so important—my health.

3. Self-care stopped because I was consumed with worry and doubt.

4. I lacked *self-awareness* about how my thoughts and feelings made me feel stuck and unable to do what mattered to me.

The more you develop self-awareness, the more you can recognize unhelpful thoughts and feelings and understand how they affect your behavior. Such awareness can allow you to detach from these thoughts, feelings, and behavior patterns, allowing you to focus on your core values and purpose.

As a result, you can more easily set and pursue goals aligned with what truly matters to you. Furthermore, self-awareness helps you uncover the root causes of stress (often your own thoughts, feelings, and behaviors), enabling you to implement effective stress management strategies. When you're able to manage stress, break free from limiting thoughts and feelings, and take committed action toward your goals, you begin to have a positive impact on those around you. Suddenly, influencing others isn't hard at all, it comes naturally. With this influence, your inner leader is unlocked. Others see that you are reliable and capable of navigating challenges as they arise.

That's been my journey to level up my influence. And, today, I want to help others do the same.

What Is Leveling Up?

Leveling up is about maximizing growth. It's about unlocking your potential, breaking free from obstacles that hold you back, and reaching new heights. Whether you're struggling to stay where you are or you're eyeing that next level of success, there's always room for growth.

Leveling up is a way of thinking. It's being authentic, intentional, and strategic. It's about knowing yourself and listening to yourself. It's about doing things that matter to you and pushing yourself out of your comfort zone—even if it scares you.

Leveling up is understanding that no matter what level you are, you still have more potential and opportunities to get even better. Some days the path seems clear and you're motivated, but other days you feel trapped, stuck, hopeless, and as if that next level is out of reach. The day-to-day grind, endless thoughts of comparison, doubting yourself, and anxiety about what's to come act as concrete barriers to keeping going.

> When you level up, your growth and influence expand, allowing your inner leader to shine naturally.

The Connection Between Self-Awareness and Influence

My clients and many of those whom I interviewed for this book likewise struggled with leveling up.

As a DJ in the EDM world, Caine found himself in a rut that he didn't know if he could get out of. Racing thoughts like, "I'll never make it because the big radio stations won't play my music," or "no venues will pay me what I'm worth so I'm not getting gigs," plagued him, crushing his creativity and motivation. The level up felt unattainable—until he realized there was something in his control that could change his career.

As a psychologist living in LA, Therese was living under the shadow of her parents' and society's expectations. She felt stifled and unhappy by this intense, constant pressure. Professionally, she was part of a community that didn't support her progressive ideas. Her level up breakthrough came when she decided to listen to herself and realized the power of influence comes from within. As a result, she moved to Europe, carved out a following as a digital nomad (at a time when this was unheard of), and became a thought leader and influencer who's living the life of her dreams.

Founding a nonprofit organization was an uphill battle for Shirley. She didn't know how to start a nonprofit but she worked tirelessly to learn what was needed. But as the organization grew, she worked harder and longer and her life became less and less balanced. Her level up was making organizational changes to better balance her personal and professional life. Fast forward to today, both her and her organization are thriving. Her nonprofit, LUCA, has enrolled over 300 students in its scholars' program and has helped over 7,000 students and parents receive support with the college process. Shirley now has a support staff of over a dozen employees, giving her time to focus on what's most important to her: LUCA's growth strategy and her family.

As you level up and reach new goals, your influence also grows. People start to hear you and actually listen. With each new level there are a new set of challenges, but also the opportunity to grow and expand your influence.

What Is Influence?

Influence, as defined by psychologist and executive coach Bill Berman, is "the indirect or intangible effect you have on others, based on what you do, how you do it, how you communicate it, and who you are."[1] It is the ability to have a powerful effect on someone or something.

---

1 Berman, William H, and George B Bradt. 2021. *Influence and Impact : Discover and Excel at What Your Organization Needs from You the Most.* Hoboken, New Jersey: Wiley.

Your influence can change people in important ways—it can motivate, inspire, or teach someone, even when this may not be your direct intention. While influence can be either positive or negative, when I talk about "leveling up your influence," I'm referring to changing others in a *positive* way. For influence to have a profound effect on others, it must be ethically and responsibly.

Leadership and influence are closely related; effective leadership is built on the ability to inspire and guide others through influence (not authority). And, as you build self-awareness and change your relationship with your thoughts and feelings, your leadership influence expands and you are able to level up.

"Why Don't I Have Influence?"

Like Caine, Therese, and Shirley, we are professionals with big aspirations and dreams of living up to our potential. At the same time, we struggle with stress, fear, anxiety, doubt— when we're unaware of these thoughts and feelings, they get in the way.

Let's look at stress. Your ability to have influence is directly tied to your ability to manage stress and your emotions. How you manage internal and external stress is key to having positive influence. If you have trouble managing stress, it can become hard to grow or influence others.

Inner obstacles such as anxiety and self-doubt can detract from the influence we aspire to have. If left unmanaged, these unhelpful thoughts and feelings can stall the pursuit of our goals and purpose.

There may be warning signs that inner obstacles are preventing you from having influence. For example:

→ Are you having a hard time getting things done?
→ Is negative self-talk a consistent distraction?
→ Are you easily annoyed?
→ Do you have trouble making decisions?
→ Do you have trouble consistently taking steps toward your goals?
→ Are you procrastinating or avoiding important tasks?
→ Is stress affecting you physically – do you have muscle tension, fatigue, or other stress-related symptoms such as headaches or stomach upset?

Whatever inner obstacles are getting in the way of your growth and goals, the way forward depends entirely on your *self-awareness.*

What Is Self-Awareness?

Self-awareness is the ability to see your strengths and areas for growth in your personal and professional lives. It is the ability to evaluate your words and actions as well as considering their impact on others. Self-awareness is essential to the development of emotional intelligence. However, inner obstacles can derail your path to self-awareness.

We all have inner obstacles or unhelpful thoughts and mindsets, but not all of us are aware of how these can block us from pursuing our passions and reaching our goals. For some, such thoughts cause them to give up and not make changes. Thinking "I'll never be good at public speaking" can cause you to avoid evaluating your current public speaking skills and identifying areas for improvement.

Unhelpful feelings can also impact our engagement in personal growth and may slow the path to self-awareness. Fear and anxiety can deter or halt progress toward your goals. For example, doubting your abilities can cause you to avoid self-reflection and feedback. Similar to unhelpful thoughts, unhelpful feelings can stop us in our tracks and cause us to avoid engaging in what can be a challenging process of personal growth and self-awareness.

Inner obstacles are often exaggerated and catastrophic thought patterns or fear-inducing emotional responses. They may be irrational and different from obstacles you identify with a clear-headed self-assessment of what you excel at and struggle with.

Self-awareness of inner obstacles enables you to course correct and implement tools for change. In subsequent chapters, we will explore practical tools that will help you develop your self-awareness, change unhelpful behavior patterns, realign with your purpose and values, and take steps toward your goals. These tools are a great starting point for growth and leveling up. However, many find that working with an executive coach can help to identify and facilitate growth more quickly than going it alone.

Why I Wrote this Book

In the chapters ahead, I share stories of a variety of professionals on different journeys to influence. My goal is to uncover *why* someone was stuck and how they leveled up.

My path to developing self-awareness, labeling my inner obstacles, refining my purpose, realigning with my core values, merging my purpose with my passion, and ultimately increasing my influence was not linear. There were changes in direction, bumps in the road, and periods where I was stuck. For years, I felt alone on this journey—but I've learned that everyone's path to growth and professional development is usually filled with different changes, bumps, and *stuck*ness.

In writing *Level Up Your Influence*, I was driven by a powerful realization: the experience of feeling stuck in a pattern of thoughts and feelings is far more common than we often talk about. Through my work with clients and conversations with colleagues, I've become more aware that this struggle is a shared human experience.

Many high achievers and successful business leaders wrestle with internal challenges, often in silence. With this in mind, I share my personal story in addition to the journeys of others who have experienced similar obstacles. My goal is to normalize these experiences, offer hope, and empower you to use psychology-based strategies and approaches that have worked for others to break free from limiting thoughts and feelings.

I interviewed other influencers and leaders from a wide variety of industries to talk about their professional journeys, the similarities and the differences, and the strategies they used to triumph over obstacles and merge their purpose with their passion. From creative fields, to professional services, to helping professions, the interviewees had similar paths to self-awareness and leveling up. In addition to the strategies that work for others, we'll dive into a psychology-based guide (the 4-Square Model) that you can use to overcome inner obstacles, increase your influence, and unlock your inner leader.

CHAPTER 2

PSYCHOLOGY-BASED COACHING

"Coaching requires knowledge of psychology and adult development, and while coaches don't have to be psychologists to be effective, it certainly helps."

TED BILILIES, PHD[2]

"David" was a C-suite leader of a tech startup who was extremely passionate about his purpose (helping others with the use of technology) and laser-focused on quality—but he failed to take breaks and listen to his people. Although he was passionate about the mission of the orga-

---

2 Bililies, Ted, PhD. 2020. "Hiring an Executive Coach? Be Aware of These Five Risks." ChiefExecutive.Net. January 15, 2020. https://chiefexecutive.net/hiring-an-executive-coach-be-aware-of-these-five-risks/.

nization, anxious thoughts and the fear of failure got in the way of him focusing on the needs and goals of his employees. These powerful inner obstacles also caused him to ignore self-care in the relentless pursuit of doing things perfectly. David didn't realize that his thoughts were the obstacle that prevented him from taking into consideration all of what he cared about.

In our coaching sessions together, David told me about how his people viewed his failure to fully listen to their needs as not caring about them. They experienced increased stress from his non-stop, frenetic pace. He was surprised by the views of his employees, because he considered himself a purpose-driven leader who cared about people and results. But his behavior said otherwise.

Through our work together, his self-awareness increased, and he was able to uncover the many thoughts that caused him to work relentlessly and ignore his self-care and listen to his employees. He realized that anxious and perfectionist thoughts prevented him from taking breaks and genuinely listening to his team.

Increasing his self-awareness of his thoughts and the behaviors they led to along with re-evaluating what mattered to him (in addition to his purpose), enabled him to set goals that included his values and purpose. David, for the first time, was able to see the big picture, and take committed action toward his goals of active listening, utilizing the strengths of each team member, and beginning to implement a self-care routine.

After several months, David's employees saw the changes and so did he. Employees reported feeling valued and started to look up to David as a leader who valued his mission and purpose along with his employees and himself. David recognized his anxious thoughts but they no longer ruled his behavior or caused him to ignore his own needs and the needs of his staff. His employees trusted him and began to view him as a role model. As a result, his influence as a leader increased. He and his employees were happier, everyone was more engaged in pursuing the company's mission, and company revenue increased.

What Is Psychology-Based Coaching?

The field of psychology provides a framework for understanding human behavior, motivation, and personality. The field of coaching often draws on these frameworks to help you develop self-awareness, change behaviors, and grow.

Psychology and coaching have several shared goals, including enhancing self-awareness, well-being, emotional intelligence, building resilience, and facilitating mindset shifts. However, most coaches don't have doctoral-level training in psychology, let alone any formal training in psychology, while others complete brief coaching programs lasting only a few months that barely scratch the surface of psychological research and principles.

Coaching psychologists have thousands of hours of training and years of coursework in the nuances of personality and behavior change. They also have a deep understanding of the ways in which behavior is affected by situations or context. Coaching psychologists' knowledge of the complex interplay between personality, behavior, and context allow them to facilitate self-awareness, growth, and lasting change in clients.

What's Wrong with a One-Size-Fits-All Approach to Coaching?

We each bring a unique set of experiences, personality traits, and biological make-up to our professional lives. As a result, a one-size-fits-all coaching program used by some coaches doesn't work for everyone. We often need more individualized guidance to leverage our unique skills and identify our areas for development. Learning skills can be helpful, but determining which skills to implement and when, as well as following through on implementation and addressing unique challenges, is much more complex.

Individual coaching that is customized takes into consideration the unique differences of the person and the situations or context that influence their behaviors. The unique characteristics of each leader affect their leadership style; their leadership style is influenced by their personality, patterns of behavior, motives, and values. In addition, each leader's organizational setting and each professional's industry brings different challenges. This context is constantly evolving and changing as the organization shifts. These shifts can include growth, restructuring, crisis, market changes, and personnel changes.

A *customized* approach to executive coaching is necessary to address the ever-evolving nuances and changes in the business world and to take into consideration the individual differences in personality and experience of each client. Additionally, when working in an organization, executive coaches seek to understand the organizational context through observation and engagement with others in the organization. While it is helpful to hear the leader's perspective on the challenges, executive coaches also interview others in the organization to develop a deeper understanding of the unique contextual variables.

Why Is the Best Coaching Psychology-Based?

Psychology provides an evidence-based human understanding of behavior to help coaching facilitate personal transformation. And as a result, coaches with advanced training and depth of knowledge in psychological principles can provide more impactful coaching services and results.

Advanced, doctoral-level training in psychology involves thousands of hours of training that develops various skills at an expert level. Key elements of this training include:

→ Deep listening skills involving years of practice using active listening, asking thoughtful questions, and reflecting back insights to facilitate self-awareness.

→ A scientific approach to assessing strengths and weaknesses using psychological tools that are both reliable and valid. Evidence-based frameworks to understand the client and organization that drive measurable growth.

→ Behavioral expertise that includes a deep understanding of motivation, emotional intelligence, communication styles, cognitive biases and other behaviors essential for leadership and business success.

→ A holistic and objective view of the client and organization. Psychologists understand the mind-body connection and the environmental variables that affect leaders and business owners.

As a result of training in these elements, psychologists are in a unique position to understand people, how they get stuck, and how they can grow their influence. They can see underlying roadblocks that would otherwise be missed by the client or those around them. And, psychologists are trained to facilitate the development of self-awareness in a non-judgmental way. Uncovering these roadblocks increases self-awareness, helps clients take action toward their goals, and allows their influence to grow.

Why Do Many Coaches Cherry-Pick from Psychology?

Most coaches (if not all) cherry-pick from psychology. Many coach training programs include some basics of psychology, and even coaches who don't have formal training pick specific ideas and frameworks and apply them haphazardly for clients. Unfortunately, all coaches don't have the training to know what strategies and frameworks to cherry pick from and when to apply them to each individual situation.

Some coaches apply the same framework to every client, which often ignores the underlying causes of behavior and the context in which the behavior occurs, making some leaders feel more stuck. In worst-case scenarios, coaches lacking advanced training in psychology can miss crucial mental health issues that will prevent leaders from reaching their goals until they are addressed.

For the purposes of this book, I'm "cherry-picking" when I discuss ACT and the 4-Square Model, but I do so as a psychologist and with the knowledge that I use many other psychology-based tools to help coaching clients (but which are beyond the scope of this book).

The Bottom Line on Coaches and Psychology

All of us can take some concepts from psychology and apply them to our professional and personal lives to help us achieve our goals. For example, everyone can benefit from using the ACT approach. But, you may have also had the experience of talking with a friend who uses one approach or strategy, applies it to everything, and tells you to just do what they did. If you've been in this situation and applied your friend's advice, it may or may not have been helpful for you in your situation.

If you had the same conversation with an experienced executive coach, the coach has some knowledge about a full set of tools, listens to you (your strengths and challenges), and adapts their approach based on your situation. A well-trained coaching psychologist is skilled in fully understanding your personality, behavior patterns, and the situation (context) to help you find the right subset of tools that work for you.

As Dr. Steven Berglas, notes in his Harvard Business Review article, "The Very Real Dangers of Executive Coaching," "Executive coaches who lack rigorous psychological training do more harm than good. By dint of their backgrounds and biases, they downplay or simply ignore deep-seated psychological problems they don't understand. Even more concerning, when an executive's problems stem from undetected or ignored psychological difficulties, coaching can actually make a bad situation worse."[3]

Coaching with the right coach can help you get to your goals faster. However, be wary of any coach that says there's only one way forward—because the one-size-fits-all approach rarely works for everyone.

Acceptance and Commitment Training (ACT)

In my career as a successful clinical psychologist, I've attended many trainings and bootcamps to hone my skills. Perhaps the most significant training I ever attended was in Acceptance and Commitment Therapy (ACT).

I went in with the desire to learn a new way for my clinical clients to deal with anxiety and depression. But, I quickly learned that ACT could be used by everyone and was effective in coaching (when referred to as Acceptance and Commitment *Training*). I walked out profoundly transformed: Here

---

3 Berglas, Steven. 2002. "The Very Real Dangers of Executive Coaching." Harvard Business Review. June 1, 2002. https://hbr.org/2002/06/the-very-real-dangers-of-executive-coaching.

was a tool, ACT, that allowed me to break free from fear, follow my purpose, and make a significant career leap.

Built upon the tenets of Cognitive Behavioral Therapy (CBT), both Acceptance and Commitment Therapy and Acceptance and Commitment Training aim to help people get *unstuck from difficult thoughts and feelings that take them away from their goals.*

Most importantly, ACT helps to:

- increase your *awareness* of unhelpful thoughts and feelings
- *interact differently* with unhelpful thoughts and feelings
- *identify* your values and goals, and
- *take action* toward your goals even when these thoughts and feelings (inner obstacles) show up
- develop a *flexible* approach to inner obstacles, uncertainty, and challenging situations (psychological flexibility).

What is ACT?

Psychologist, Russ Harris, simplifies ACT using the following acronym:

- A = Accept your thoughts and feelings, and be present
- C = Choose a valued direction
- T = Take action[4]

4 Harris, Russ. 2009. ACT Made Simple: An Easy-To-Read Primer on Acceptance and Commitment Therapy. https://ci.nii.ac.jp/ncid/BB04378809.

ACT provides a framework for understanding the obstacles that show up for you that can get in the way of your goals. These obstacles are both internal (your thoughts and feelings) and external (behaviors). This framework helps you identify obstacles, change your relationship with them, and continue to take steps toward goals that matter most to you. It also helps you remain grounded in your values and align your values with your goals.

The goal of ACT is to help you take action in the direction of your values or what matters most to you. In practice, it helps increase your awareness of and navigate thoughts and feelings that can get in the way of our goals. ACT helps you to develop psychological flexibility—the ability to respond more effectively to life's challenges including inner obstacles, maintain well-being, and live a life that is more aligned with your values.

While ACT has been researched as an effective treatment for diagnosable clinical conditions such as anxiety and depression, and there is evidence of ACT's effectiveness in reducing chronic pain and treating trauma, the ACT framework has been modified to help the non-clinical population.

ACT can help anyone struggling to reach a personal or professional goal. Additionally, ACT has enormous value in leadership development. For the purposes of this book, the use of ACT will refer to Acceptance and Commitment Training, an evidence-based approach that helps people keep moving in the direction of their goals even when obstacles arise.

At its most basic, ACT is about increasing self-awareness of difficult thoughts and feelings and their influence on your behavior; it encompasses accepting that these thoughts and feelings will show up, but that you still take committed actions toward your goals.

ACT, essentially, is a guide to increasing self-awareness, maximizing growth, and unlocking your inner leader. Let's dive into its key elements.

Acceptance

Elements of Western mindfulness are incorporated into ACT. Mindfulness was adopted from Eastern philosophies such as Buddhism. However, unlike Buddhism, mindfulness has no religious elements.

In Acceptance and Commitment Therapy, mindfulness strategies are incorporated into the acceptance component. Acceptance begins with exercises around noticing and observing your thoughts and behaviors.

The practice of observing yourself – your thoughts and behaviors – helps to develop self-awareness around what thoughts and feelings get in your way. Once you have the skills of noticing and accepting, the next step is engaging in activities that align with your values.

What Is Mindfulness?

Mindfulness has become popular in the United States over the past several years. However, the roots of mindfulness date back thousands of years to Buddhism philosophy. Removing the religious elements from mindfulness, Jon Kabat-Zinn, an American professor and researcher, developed a program in the late 1970s called mindfulness-based stress reduction (MBSR) to help people cope with chronic pain and illness.

Kabat-Zinn defines mindfulness as, "awareness that arises through paying attention, on purpose, in the present moment, non-judgmentally."[5] His work demonstrated the effectiveness of mindfulness in improving mental and physical health.

Being mindful means you are fully present in the moment. You are aware of what you are doing and the experience of what you are doing. You are engaged in the activity and not focused on thoughts of the future or the past. You may have noticed that you are mindful when you are learning something new and giving it your full attention. You are completely immersed in the activity, aware of what you see and hear, and not bogged down by thoughts of the past or worry about the future.

Mindfulness is a key component of ACT and a tool for stress management. Mindfulness can be described as the act of being present and engaging

---

5 Mindful Staff. 2019. "Jon Kabat-Zinn: Defining Mindfulness - Mindful." Mindful. January 11, 2019. https://www.mindful.org/jon-kabat-zinn-defining-mindfulness/.

all of your senses. It is a skill requiring observation of all five senses as well as learning to observe thoughts and feelings.

The practice of observing your thoughts and feelings and where they show up for you physically (i.e., you feel anxiety in your chest) increases your awareness of what's happening in the here and now. By noticing your thoughts and feelings, you can get space from their intensity, which allows you to make more objective decisions during times of stress and allows you to focus on your goals.

Commitment

Commitment to your goals is something that most of us struggle with at some point. We may identify and set goals but then have trouble consistently taking steps toward them. Unhelpful thoughts and feelings can easily become obstacles to staying committed to your goals if you're not aware of them and haven't practiced accepting them.

What are you committing to and what are you committing to it? Before you can truly commit to taking action, you need to know the why behind it. Asking yourself questions like who and what matters to me is a great starting point before setting goals. Answering these questions or conducting a values assessment to identify your core values can help you develop goals and actions that are aligned with both your values and purpose. The goal is to uncover what is important to you and then identify what it looks like when doing those things. These behaviors are the actions you commit to taking. When others see you engaging in behaviors that align with your values, your influence naturally increases.

The ACT Matrix, AKA The 4-Square Model

In my psychology-based coaching, the ACT Matrix tool is one of the most helpful in getting us unstuck and taking action toward increasing our influence. The ACT matrix was designed as an easier, more user-friendly way to explain ACT theory.

Because the ACT matrix is divided into four squares, I like to refer to it as the *4-Square Model*. The 4-Square Model serves as a guide to maximizing your growth, leveling up your influence, and allowing your inner leader to shine. Using the 4-Square Model increases your self-awareness by helping you to identify obstacles to growth, identify goals, and take action toward your goals even when these obstacles are present.

The 4 squares of the ACT matrix include your internal world (thoughts, feelings, values) and your external world (behaviors that others can see). The bottom two squares describe your inner world which includes what you care about, and unhelpful thoughts and feelings you experience. The top two squares represent your actions or behaviors and are the things you do in response to your inner experience. Starting from the bottom and looking inside can be helpful in understanding your own behaviors. If you think about an iceberg, the top two squares are above the water (what people can see) and the bottom two squares are beneath the water (what others can't see but that serve as the foundation for your behaviors).

The squares on the left side of the page comprise your unhelpful thoughts and feelings (bottom left square) and what you do when you get hooked or stuck from these thoughts and feelings (top left square). The squares on the right side of the page include your values and who and what is important to you (bottom right square) and what you do when you are acting toward your values (top right square).

Because our inner thoughts and feelings drive our actions, it's helpful to start by examining them first. ACT coaches may explore the matrix with clients using different starting points but typically start with your values and what is important to you. ACT therapists typically start examining the matrix with a client by looking at unhelpful thoughts and feelings.

The 4-Square Model, Visualized

For the purposes of this book, the 4-Square Model is presented starting with unhelpful thoughts and feelings, as I've found starting here is most user-friendly for readers. (Most of us can easily identify thoughts and feelings that are unhelpful).

The 4-Square Model begins with you in the middle of the page with four arrows; an arrow pointing above you, below you, to the right, and to the left. As a result, the page is divided into four quadrants or squares.

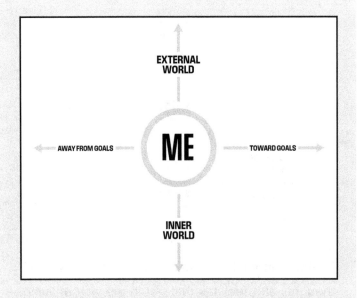

- The bottom two squares represent your inner world (thoughts, feelings, values, and purpose) and the top two squares represent the external world (your behaviors).
- The right two squares help you move toward your goals and the left two squares move you away from your goals.

Square 1: Unhelpful Thoughts and Feelings

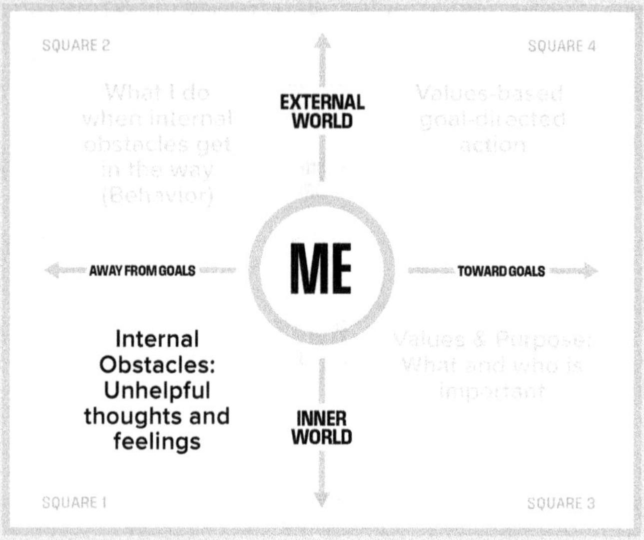

SQUARE 2

What I do when internal obstacles get in the way (Behavior)

EXTERNAL WORLD

SQUARE 4

Values-based goal-directed action

←···· **AWAY FROM GOALS** ···· **ME** ····· **TOWARD GOALS** ·····→

Internal Obstacles: Unhelpful thoughts and feelings

INNER WORLD

Values & Purpose: What and who is important

SQUARE 1

SQUARE 3

In the bottom left square, you write down the thoughts and feelings that get in the way of living out your values or completing the actions in the top right box. Take a moment and draw the four squares on a piece of paper like the above diagram and in the bottom left square write down unhelpful thoughts or feelings that you have about yourself that get in your way. These can be negative, irrational, or extreme thoughts that you have to do things perfectly or thoughts that you will always fail or never be good enough. Write down the first few that come to mind. For example, Matt has the thought that he won't ever succeed at starting his own business and he feels sad and anxious.

Square 2: What I Do When Unhelpful Thoughts and Feelings Show Up

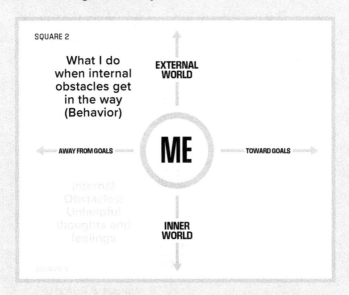

In the top left square, jot down the answer to the following question, "What do I do when I have this thought or feeling?" Do you doom scroll on TikTok, have a drink, go to sleep? For instance, when Matt has the thought that that he won't ever succeed at starting his own business, he binge watches Netflix to distract himself from those thoughts and to avoid feeling sad and anxious (making him avoid spending time developing a business plan). This box should be a list of things you do when unhelpful thoughts and feelings show up. Many people say they do nothing when they experience these thoughts and feelings. And while this may feel true, you are likely not doing something productive, but you are doing something that is less productive or not helping you reach your goals. The purpose of this box is to write down what you are doing that another person can see such as watching TV or doom scrolling.

Square 3: Values and Purpose

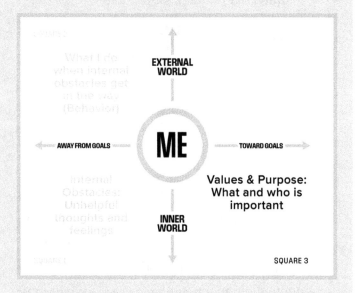

In the third square, make a list of your values—the things you care about and the people you care about (including yourself). A great way to start this list is by asking yourself, "Who and what is important to you?" Also include in this square your purpose or your why. Returning to the example of Matt, he identified what was important to him: working for himself and bringing his innovative idea to the world and his purpose was to help others solve a problem with his idea.

Square 4: Committed Actions Toward Values

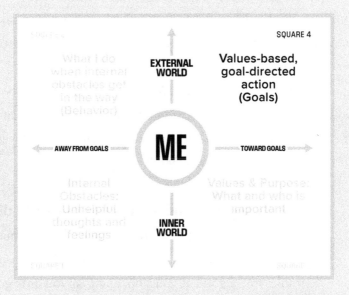

Once you have completed square 3, in the top right square (square 4) write down what people can see you doing to know what your values and purpose are. This can include goals you are working toward that are aligned with your values and purpose. For example, Matt's goal was to start his own business and identified the steps of developing a business plan, networking with other professionals, and finding a mentor.

How Can the 4-Square Model Help Me?

The 4-Square Model can be used as a framework to help you increase self-awareness, improve decision-making, align with purpose, double-down on values-based behaviors, and take action towards your goals. Developing each of these skills leads to growth, increased influence, and leadership.

For instance, the 4-Square Model can be applied both to your overall job and to specific tasks such as a high-pressure meeting or having a difficult conversation with an employee.

To complete a 4-Square Model for your job:

1. **Identify thoughts and feelings that can get in the way of what's important.** For example, you may think that you are not good at your job, that no one thinks you're good at your job, and that you only got a promotion because you were lucky.

2. **List things you might do when those feelings come up that cause you to get stuck.** For example, you might put off completing work-related tasks and read a book to distract yourself from these unhelpful thoughts.

3. **Ask yourself who and what is important in this work situation.** Is completing work tasks important? Is engaging with your co-workers important? Is providing feedback important? Is completing undesirable tasks important?

4. **Identify what people see you doing that shows who and what is important.** For example, if completing work tasks is important, others may see you implementing a plan of action steps to complete tasks.

To prepare for a situation, you can complete a matrix the same way prior to entering the situation. Just complete these 4 steps in relation to the specific situation. Doing so can enable you to see where you might get stuck and identify behaviors that you want to engage in during the situation.

For example, in a difficult conversation with an employee, getting stuck might look like thoughts of feeling uncomfortable with conflict resulting in avoiding talking about the employee's failure to meet multiple deadlines. However, your values may indicate that you care about this employee and can show you care (committed action) by using active listening skills including asking open-ended questions.

Level Up with the 4-Square Model as Your Guide

After years of wanting to start a consulting practice but being blocked by thoughts "You can't do it" and fear of failing, the 4-Square Model helped me decide to take this big career leap. I knew exactly what I wanted to do and I knew that I wouldn't allow limiting thoughts and feelings to keep me from making it happen. However, I struggled with creating a clear path for starting this new and different type of business.

Given that my training as a clinical psychologist required that I receive therapy for several hundred hours, I decided that it made sense that if I was going to be an executive coach, I should work with one and experience the benefits from the client side.

At the time, I didn't know what to expect, but working with an executive coach skyrocketed my business into existence. I chose to work with a coaching psychologist who helped me to uncover strengths I didn't know I had and leverage them to develop my business. She also helped me through our conversations and personality testing, identifying areas for growth. In addition, our coaching sessions were motivating and they provided accountability for the goals I set. I found that I often exceeded the goals. My path to self-awareness during the process was exponential and Shaping Success was born.

The process of psychology-based coaching facilitates the development of self-awareness—or as some people say "holding up the mirror." Using the 4-Square Model is a guide that you can use to hold up the mirror without having an executive coach. This guide can jumpstart the continuous path to self-awareness that is necessary for leveling up your influence and maximizing your potential.

Mindfulness and acceptance enable you to free yourself from getting stuck as a result of difficult thoughts and feelings. Mindfulness gives you space from the emotion and acceptance of judgmental thoughts that can stop you from moving towards your goals. When we are aware of our thoughts and feelings, we can implement the practice of mindful acceptance. This increases your ability to make sound decisions, often leading to better results, more confidence and increases your credibility and trust; all of which level up your influence and lead to growth.

The 4-Square Model is a guide to self-awareness that will help you break free from thoughts and feelings that hold you back from reaching your goals. It will become your go-to guide for leveling up your influence, maximizing your growth, and unlocking your inner leader. The benefits of using this guide are two-fold—skyrocketing your career goals and leadership, and navigating roadblocks and challenging situations.

This guide, combined with the strategies used by successful business leaders, influencers, and creatives to level up, will arm you with all of the tools you need to level up your influence and achieve your dreams.

PART II

YOUR SELF-AWARENESS GUIDE

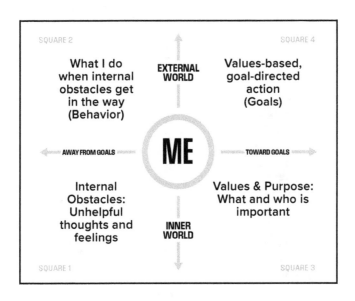

Ch. 3: Square #1: Identifying Internal Obstacles: Unhelpful Thoughts and Feelings

Ch. 4: Square #2: What Happens When Internal Obstacles Get in the Way?

Ch. 5: Square #3: Values and Purpose

Ch. 6: Square #4: Values-Based, Goal-Directed Action

Ch. 7: Influence, Leveled Up

CHAPTER 3

SQUARE #1: IDENTIFYING INTERNAL OBSTACLES: UNHELPFUL THOUGHTS AND FEELINGS

> *"You are not your thoughts. You are the one who observes your thoughts."*
> – ECKART TOLLE

Sam (whose name has been changed for confidentiality purposes) had a 9 to 5 job in sales that he didn't care about but dreamed of being a successful DJ and playing in front of thousands of fans. He loved Electronic Dance Music (EDM) and aspired to make and play music like Martin Garrix. However, it felt like a pipe dream. How would he get there? There were so many other talented DJs out there—why would anyone want to hear him play? It felt like his dream would never become a reality.

He continued his 9 to 5, spent little time practicing his DJ skills, and put his dreams on hold because he thought it was impossible. Sam didn't create a plan or engage in activities that would further his DJ career aside from inconsistent practice. This continued until one day, something changed. After talking to another DJ and reflecting on his own path, he realized that his mindset was holding him back from even trying. Thoughts like, "I'll never be as good as Martin Garrix," and "I don't have what it takes to be a great DJ," and "It's impossible to be a good DJ while working a full-time job," were stopping him before he even started. This moment of self-awareness was triggered by a conversation with a fellow DJ who had a similar experience. However, he didn't know how to change these thoughts and he had no plan of how to become a full time DJ. Sam felt completely stuck.

Sam decided to talk to his best friend about this dilemma. His friend had the solution immediately and said "You need to work with a coach. It changed the way I view my work and helped me improve my P & L." He was an analyst in a hedge fund and working with an executive coach helped him to think about his job differently, and, as a result, he was able to stop letting his thoughts get in the way of both his performance and leading his team. As a result, his productivity increased, he was able to motivate his team, and their overall performance increased.

Although Sam didn't fully understand how he could change his mindset, he knew he couldn't do it on his own; he needed to do something different. He felt like these thoughts had been there for years and he wasn't sure if it was possible to get rid of them. Sam hired a coach, and through the coaching process he uncovered all of the thoughts that got in the way of pursuing his passion, embracing a career as a DJ.

Sam would have these thoughts and it would cause him to avoid taking important steps toward his goals. He would skip practicing on the decks and not make time to network with other DJs and industry professionals. His coach helped him to understand that the larger goal of becoming a fulltime EDM DJ was attainable but it would require a plan with smaller goals and action steps.

Once Sam was able to notice those unhelpful thoughts and accept that they were there, he could refocus on small action steps toward his goals. This motivated him to celebrate his progress and keep going.

Sam's mindset was the biggest obstacle to growth as a DJ. He had hundreds if not thousands of unhelpful thoughts getting in his way: "I'll never be good enough," "I'll never get any gig," "They won't play my songs on the radio because I don't know people at the top." These thoughts fueled feelings of frustration, sadness, anxiety, and cynicism. And, through the coaching process, he realized that feeling frustrated or cynical about the music industry made him feel stuck and decreased his motivation to work toward his goals.

At first, Sam couldn't put his finger on what was getting in his way, but realizing and understanding that unhelpful thoughts and feelings were his biggest obstacles was the first step toward overcoming what was causing him to be stuck. Being open to an idea from a friend, and even though he didn't understand how the coaching process worked, being open to giving it a try was the key shift that sparked his self-awareness.

Sam's coach asked open-ended questions based on the 4-Square Model that helped him uncover his unhelpful thoughts and feelings. This helped him make the connection between the unhelpful thoughts and feelings and how they impacted his behaviors. Sam's unhelpful thoughts and feelings led to not thinking about what he could do to make his DJ dreams a reality. He was doing the opposite—playing video games, doom scrolling on Instagram, not learning new DJ skills, not creating a marketing strategy, and not networking.

Through talking with his coach and engaging in self-reflection, his self-awareness of these thoughts and feelings in real time increased. Uncovering these patterns and subsequently creating new patterns with his coach was a process that sometimes felt challenging but Sam started to see the changes in how he was feeling and he noticed his motivation increasing. He was taking action steps toward his goals, which further motivated him to keep going on this new path.

Self-Awareness: The First Step

Self-awareness is the ability to see your strengths and areas for growth in your personal and professional lives. It is the ability to evaluate your words, actions, thoughts, and feelings as well as considering their impact on others. Self-awareness is essential to the development of emotional regulation, i.e., being able to recognize your emotions and not let them control your actions and decision-making. However, inner obstacles can derail your path to self-awareness.

Like Sam, we all have unhelpful thoughts and mindsets, but not all of us are aware of how these thoughts can block us from pursuing our passions and reaching our goals. For some, these thoughts cause them to give up and not make changes. For instance, thoughts such as "I'll never be good at public speaking," can cause you to avoid public speaking instead of evaluating your current public speaking skills and identifying areas for improvement.

Unhelpful feelings can also impact our engagement in professional and personal growth, slowing the path to self-awareness. Fear and anxiety can deter or halt progress toward our goals. For example, doubt about your abilities can cause you to avoid self-reflection and feedback. Similar to unhelpful thoughts, unhelpful feelings can stop us in our tracks and cause us to avoid engaging in what can be a challenging process of personal growth and self-awareness. Developing self-awareness of unhelpful thoughts is the first step to leveling up your influence and moving in the direction of your goals.

What is EDM?

Electronic Dance Music refers to a broad category of music that uses electronic instruments or other technology to create sounds that are designed to be played at nightclubs, raves, and festivals. Over time, the EDM genre has grown to include over a dozen subgenres such as progressive house, tropical house, drum and base, dubstep, and techno.

Why is the EDM Career Trajectory a Struggle for Many DJs?

Differing from local club or wedding DJs, an aspiring EDM DJ not only plays music but also produces music and has very different career goals. EDM DJs typically start by developing their skills in music production and DJ techniques, often releasing tracks on smaller labels or independently and playing local gigs. Depending on the EDM DJ, they may first start with developing DJ skills or they may first focus on production skills and releasing music. As they grow their audience and develop their brand, they build their network and/or work with a booking agent to land performances at larger clubs and smaller festival stages, while continuing to release music and potentially collaborating with established artists. While continuing to grow their audience through their music and performances, they can progress to playing at major festivals, headlining shows, and eventually performing at world-renowned music festivals, all while maintaining a consistent output of music releases. Many EDM DJs also launch their own record label and build a team to support their growth. An EDM DJ's team often includes the positions of manager, booking agent, public relations specialist, social media manager, tour manager, and sound engineer.

Psychology-Based Coaching for EDM DJs

When I work with EDM DJs, I'm often helping them with the psychology behind their brand, performance, and business. Understanding the impact of their inner obstacles or mindset challenges on progress toward their goals is a key step to reaching their DJ aspirations. When I partner with each DJ, we develop a customized plan with actions steps to tackle different areas such as developing networking and communication skills, maintaining consistency in different areas such as social media or production, handling rejection, prioritizing wellness, dealing with stress, navigating industry politics, managing mindset challenges, and building an authentic brand.

Inner Obstacles

On your journey to achieving your aspirations and reaching your goals, you will inevitably encounter inner obstacles—the thoughts and feelings that get in the way of progress. Becoming aware of these mental roadblocks and then labeling them as "inner obstacles" are the first steps to addressing how you get in your own way which can help you forge a path forward.

Unhelpful Thoughts

On any given day, we have thousands and thousands of thoughts. Our thoughts can help or hinder us from moving toward our goals. Thoughts may be categorized as rational or irrational, positive or negative, helpful or unhelpful but they often influence our behavior. And, situations can trigger our thoughts. Unhelpful thoughts are one of two large buckets of inner obstacles.

Marla's story

Who am I to go on Instagram live to talk about my day? Why do 11,000 people care about me?

Marla Beth Enowitz is an influencer and artist known for her signature "happy art." Baseline anxiety has been a part of her life since she was young. To deal with it, she learned to apply tools such as pushing herself beyond her comfort zone, keeping her purpose top of mind and celebrating her progress.

But being a social media influencer with a huge audience came with its own kind of anxiety, the kind when an artist puts it all out there on social media and risks rejection and criticism. When I interviewed Marla for this book, she described the anxiety as, "an out of body experience that felt like a wave," that was attached to so many thoughts like "How is this happening to me?" and "Why do I deserve any special attention?"

Marla's overwhelming feelings and thoughts easily could have caused her to avoid posting on social media—but remembering her purpose was one thing that helped. She describes her art as "happy, inclusive, and a community." Having a strong "why" helped Marla to keep sharing her art with the world and making content.

Unhelpful thoughts have gotten in the way for me and most of my clients. I've seen many people give up on their dreams or put pursuing them on the back burner and I've done this myself. Wanting to pursue a new direction but having the unhelpful thought that I couldn't do it prevented me from making a career shift for many years.

While each client may have a varying awareness of the impairment that inner obstacles of thoughts and feelings have, our discussions have often brought to light the role that anxious thoughts and feelings play in task completion or avoidance.

Increasing self-awareness of inner obstacles and the connection between thoughts, feelings, and behaviors is a core part of the work I do with clients. Once this connection is understood, it becomes easier to understand how they can derail you from your goals and refocus on engaging in behaviors that are aligned with their goals. This process is part of taking committed action towards goals in Acceptance and Commitment Training.

Thoughts Get in the Way

When the going gets tough, how do we respond? It's no surprise that the way we *act* is determined by the way we *think*. And if we're thinking negatively, it'll get in the way of our actions. Thoughts have immense power over our behavior.

Critical or anxious thoughts, judgments, and doubts can derail us from moving toward our goals. These are the thoughts described in the 4-Square Model's bottom left box as unhelpful thoughts that move us away from our goals.

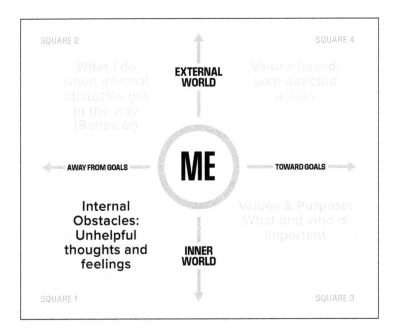

Unhelpful thoughts are often related to the following feelings:

- Self-doubt
- Anxiety
- Anger

What Is Self-Doubt?

Self-doubt is when you question your abilities and skills. It can stem from fear of failure or lack of experience. Sometimes, self-doubt can be fleeting and can decrease as your experience and competence increase, but sometimes it remains and can become an inner obstacle that holds you back from accomplishing your goals. Related to self-doubt, but often more intense, is imposter syndrome. Imposter syndrome is a term used to describe feeling like a fraud despite actual accomplishments. The inability to accept successes as a result of competence and attribute successes to external factors is part of this psychological phenomenon and can become a debilitating inner obstacle.

How Does Self-Doubt Impact Me?

Self-doubt can become an inner obstacle and affect your behavior; you may delay making decisions, avoid completing tasks, or not make a career leap. Self-doubt can decrease your confidence and lead to feeling bad about yourself.

How Does Self-Doubt Show Up in My Professional Life

Self-doubt can impact decision-making—you may delay making important decisions, procrastinate important tasks, and fail to communicate with others. Depending on the intensity of these feelings, they can take over and lead to behaviors that get you stuck—you may stop moving toward your goals, and, at times, you may move in the opposite direction of your goals.

What is anxiety?

Anxiety is an emotional and often physical response to perceived threat or stressors that cause excessive worry or angst. This response can range in intensity and can include feelings of fear related to specific situations (e.g., flying) or be more broad (e.g., fear of failure). Physical symptoms of anxiety can include rapid heart rate, sweating, and muscle tension.

How does anxiety impact me?

Anxiety related to real or imagined situations can cause physical symptoms and it can also impact your behavior. Anxiety can lead to unhelpful thought patterns such as spiraling (negative thought pattern where one thought triggers another thought in a downward cycle) or ruminating (repetitive thoughts and overly focusing on the negative). It can show up as brain fog, where you suddenly can't seem to process information or prioritize options; it can seem to flood you, where it becomes hard to hear; or it can seem to focus your world inward rather than outward. You may avoid situations (e.g., public speaking) or not try new things (e.g., apply for a new job). You may engage in unhealthy coping mechanisms such as over-eating, binge watching a Netflix series, or drinking alcohol to ease the discomfort of anxiety.

How does anxiety show up in my professional life?

Anxiety can have a significant effect on your professional activities and success. Avoiding difficult conversations, not asking for a promotion, failing to speak up during meetings, and avoiding networking can all prevent you from reaching your professional goals. Moreover, anxiety can prevent you from setting goals and taking steps to reach them.

Unhelpful thoughts are biased or inaccurate ways of thinking that can be negative or irrational. They can fuel anxiety, doubt, and anger. While there are many types of unhelpful thoughts, here are a few more to give you a general idea of thoughts that can get in the way.

→ One common pattern is all-or-nothing thinking, where you oversimplify situations using statements such as always and never. For example, we may think "If I don't get this job, I'm a total failure" or "my boss always hates my ideas so I must be stupid."

→ Perfectionist thoughts can also involve all-or-nothing thought patterns and you may have thoughts such as,

"I can never release this song because it's not perfect", or "I'm not going to bother starting a business because I will never get everything perfectly in order for the business to be successful."

→ Another unhelpful thought pattern involves catastrophizing the worst-case scenario and magnifying the negative. For example, while writing this book, I had the thought "If I make grammar errors in my book, everyone will think I'm a careless person."

→ Attributing successes and failure to external factors is another category of unhelpful thoughts that can decrease your motivation, increase anger, and leave you feeling like there's not much in your control. For example, "I got a great performance review because my boss is a nice person and likes me (not because of my outstanding performance and list of accomplishments)."

→ Then there are thoughts where you attribute your success to luck and failure to our own shortcomings: "I got the job because the company needed to fill the position and they had no one else" or "I didn't get the job because I have no valuable skills so no one would hire me."

These thoughts and more can be unhelpful. They make it hard to see things accurately, take our values into consideration, and take actions based on our values. All unhelpful thought patterns can cause an emotional response that results in an action or inaction. Your emotional response (unhelpful feelings) often arises in response to your unhelpful thoughts. If you don't manage these feelings, they can be a major barrier to reaching your goals.

Unhelpful Feelings

"It really felt like death was an inch away from me. And any wrong move now would mean the closure of our business and likely complete financial ruin. I was faced with what was arguably a business-ending and personal financial-ruin event. All wrapped up in one."

Robert Cioffi, co-founder and co-owner of Progressive Computing and successful leader in the IT industry for over 20 years, was confronted with his worst nightmare: a cyber-attack; all of his information and the information of his clients was hacked by a cybercrime ring. Suddenly, he froze and was overcome with crippling fear. He thought he was on the brink of financial ruin and that everything he worked for decades to achieve would be lost.

It was a typical day at the office—people working at their desks, customers being helped—until Robert received a phone call. Answering this call and receiving the news of being hit by a cyber-attack felt "like being in a car wreck." He was in shock, frozen, scared, and had no idea how to respond. He felt like the collapse of his business and financial ruin was inevitable.

Ten minutes passed but he had no concept of time as he stood there immobilized until he felt a hand on his shoulder and heard the words, "We've got this." It was another one of

Robert's leaders who snapped him out of this frozen state. In that moment feeling his partner's hand, he sprang into action. He knew he had to be a tower of strength for his employees although he had no confidence, no plan, and was overwhelmed by fear. "Just do your best; just do," were thoughts he had in these moments.

Through intense fear and anxiety about the future of his business, his clients, and potential financial ruin, Robert remembered what and who was important; his clients, his employees, and his business. He decided that presence and communication were essential during this crisis. He gathered his staff together to discuss the situation and allowed them to ask questions. He worked with his partner to devise a plan.

Together, they sought support and implemented a plan that would save his business. This harrowing incident shook him to his core but the feeling of triumph that came from diving in head on and surviving increased his resilience. It also led to international speaking engagements about managing a business leader's worst nightmare and helping other businesses to prepare for the worst.

Feelings Get in the Way

Just as the power of thoughts to impact our actions or inaction, our feelings can have a gripping effect on our behavior. Thoughts impact our feelings, and our feelings can impact our thoughts. Unhelpful feelings such as anxiety can cause a physical response that can distract us from what's important.

Both thoughts and feelings can have a strong influence on behavior. Feelings are complex, nuanced, and influenced by your experiences. As a result, your thoughts and feelings can influence your decision-making negatively, causing you to avoid important tasks/decisions or make decisions based on emotions.

When your actions are guided by anxiety, self-doubt, anger, sadness or some combination of these feelings, they will likely take you in the opposite direction of your goals. Any one of these feelings can keep you from taking the next big step in your career, putting out music you created, or starting a new business.

Unhelpful feelings can cause us to engage in behaviors that prevent us from taking values-based, committed actions. They may take over and cause us to avoid doing what matters to us.

Common unhelpful feelings can be categorized into the following emotion buckets:

- → fear/anxiety
- → sadness
- → anger

It's important to note that as you examine your own feelings and start to increase your awareness of your feelings and how they impact your actions, categorizing these thoughts is not necessary. I am categorizing them here for your understanding, however you may have feelings in multiple categories. What matters is distinguishing unhelpful from helpful feelings; feelings that push you to take action toward your goals.

What Is Fear?

Fear comes from anything we perceive as a threat to our survival. When we see that a threat is present, it triggers a *physiological* response to help us eliminate or get away from the threat.

Why Do I Have Fear?

The human response to fear helped the cavemen survive. When cave people were sitting around the fire and saw a shadow of a saber-toothed tiger, they had two options – fight the tiger or run for their lives. Their bodies were suddenly thrown into fight or flight or sometimes freeze.[6]

The amygdala is the area of the brain that perceives the threat and causes the sympathetic nervous system to be activated. Once activated, it triggers symptoms such as elevated heart rate, anxiety, tensed muscles, shallow breathing, and increased oxygen flow to your major muscles. In response to the threat of danger, your body prepares to fight, run, or freeze. The fight or flight response helped the caveman stay alive in a life-or-death situation.[7]

6 Schmidt, Norman B., J. Anthony Richey, Michael J. Zvolensky, and Jon K. Maner. "Exploring human freeze responses to a threat stressor." *Journal of behavior therapy and experimental psychiatry* 39, no. 3 (2008): 292-304.

7 Šimić, Goran, Mladenka Tkalčić, Vana Vukić, Damir Mulc, Ena Španić, Marina Šagud, Francisco E. Olucha-Bordonau, Mario Vukšić, and Patrick R. Hof. "Understanding emotions: origins and roles of the amygdala." *Biomolecules* 11, no. 6 (2021): 823.

How Does Fear Impact Me?

While fight or flight was helpful in survival situations, the amygdala can't distinguish between real and perceived threats. As a result, when there is a perceived threat and the amygdala is triggered, it puts the body through unnecessary stress. For example, the stress response can be triggered by running late, presenting to a group, traffic, or your boss wanting to talk to you.

How Does Fear Show Up in My Professional Life?

Fear often causes avoidance; fear of the worst outcome can hinder your professional growth on a large scale or in smaller ways, preventing you from making bold career moves such as changing careers or engaging in activities to build your business such as networking. When you get hooked by unhelpful thoughts related to fear and anxiety, you may avoid difficult conversations or avoid making decisions. This avoidance may take you away from your mission and negatively impact the bottom line of your business. Furthermore, avoidance and indecision can erode trust, which can hinder your professional and business growth.

What is anger?

Anger is an emotional state that can vary in intensity from mild irritability to intense rage and is often in response to a negative, triggering event. Similar to anxiety, anger is often accompanied by a physical response including increased heart rate, blood pressure, and the release of adrenalin.

Why do I have anger?

Anger is also considered by many to be a secondary emotion; a reaction to more challenging emotions such as fear, anxiety, sadness, hurt, and frustration. Rather than express these more vulnerable emotions, anger can become a go-to emotional response.

However, anger is often a signal of what is important to us. Anger is often triggered when you feel wronged. For example, if someone violates your beliefs or goes against your values, anger can be a common response. You may feel anger when someone cuts you in line because you care about following the rules and believe that people should wait their turn.

How does anger impact me?

Anger can have a physical impact and an impact on your behavior. Prolonged anger is correlated with high blood pressure and increased risk for heart attack. Anger can also lead to impulsive decision-making; saying things without thinking about the consequences or other people's feelings.

How does anger show up in my professional life?

Anger can negatively impact your professional and business success. Anger can negatively affect relationships with your colleagues and customers. Making quick decisions based on anger can cloud your judgment and prevent you from seeing the big picture. This can lead to failing to consider others' feelings and failing to consider the long-term consequences of your actions, often resulting in subsequent regret. And, if you're feeling angry, you may feel like things are out of your control, and subsequently be less likely to focus on what's in your control, which is taking steps toward your goals.

Within these three larger buckets of feelings(fear/anxiety, sadness, and anger), there are many subtypes of unhelpful feelings that can be obstacles to growth. Sometimes, you may find that you identify with an emotion that falls under a subcategory of the three larger categories explained above. Here are a few common feelings to give you a general idea of the array of more specific feelings that can get in the way.

- *Dread* is feeling that the worst will happen. You may feel trapped and it can cause avoidance or procrastination. Dread can include physical symptoms such as tightness in the chest and muscle tension.
- *Sadness* can include a variety of feelings such as apathy, a lack of feeling or emotion, regret, or loneliness. With apathy, you may not actually feel sad, and rather identify more with a lack of having feeling.
- When it comes to *anger*, your experience may be more consistent with irritability, impatience, frustration, bitterness, jealousy, or envy.

If you experience trouble identifying the specific emotions you are experiencing, it can be helpful to identify situations that spark unhelpful feelings.

How Did Robert Rebound from the Hacker Attack?

Two things helped Robert to rebound from this extreme crisis: talking about it (communicating with his team and receiving support from them) and noticing (seeing his extreme emotional response and choosing to take action toward his values).

A core value that Robert instilled in his company is teamwork and a key component of teamwork is effective communication. Although he was frozen by an unhelpful emotion, intense fear, and anxiety, he realigned with his values. Remaining frozen did not embody teamwork. Remembering his values and purpose, he said to himself, "I have to be a tower of strength and the strongest leader possible." He recalled that he "had almost no confidence and no plan," but he "was going to step up to the plate and do his best."

Robert's next steps were to communicate and just start doing. He called a meeting with his team and talked about the situation, acknowledged their intense stress level, and allowed them to ask questions. Despite his anxiety, he made the phone calls to his insurance and attorneys. Based on their advice, he worked with his partner to develop an action plan.

Fast forward, Robert and his team successfully navigated the process to avoid financial ruin and retain their clients. The process was filled with uncertainty and angst, but Robert kept in mind who and what was important and used this as a guide to take action. He's gone on to speak internationally about this near disaster to help other IT professionals learn from his experience. Robert developed resilience through this experience and leveled up his influence by being a role model for handling crises and helping thousands of others to learn from his experience.

Psychology-based Self-Awareness Strategies for Unhelpful Thoughts and Feelings

Now that we've uncovered the complicated relationship between our thoughts and our actions, there are psychology-based, research-based strategies that you can start using right now that will further develop your awareness of your own thoughts and feelings, and how they impact you on a daily basis. Whether you are experiencing unhelpful thoughts, unhelpful feelings, or both simultaneously, trying any of the strategies below will help you.

Here are the top five action strategies that have helped my clients to take the reigns over the inner obstacles that hold them back from leveling up:

- Catch, Label, and Pack
- Visualization for Thoughts: "Passing Clouds"
- Visualization for Feelings: Feelings as Objects
- Self-compassion
- Talking About It: Support from others

Catch, Label, and Pack

- **Catch:** To catch is to notice your thoughts as they're coming up, bringing your attention to them as they happen. Then, using the words, "I'm noticing that," in front of the thought. For example, "I'm noticing that I'm thinking about my fear of having a difficult conversation." Continuing to notice and label your thoughts in this way can help increase your awareness of the thoughts as they're happening. A practice of "I'm noticing that X makes me think Y" can help to give you space from the thoughts and see them more objectively. You can take that a step further by saying, "I'm noticing that I'm having the thought that..." Adding this phrase can help create even more distance between you and the thoughts. Your goal is to observe the thoughts, watching them come and go without getting attached or stuck to them.

→ **Label:** Once you are able to notice your unhelpful thoughts and feelings, naming them as "inner obstacles" can help you to see them more clearly. Labeling your unhelpful thoughts and feelings that are inner obstacles, imagine writing the label "inner obstacles" on a box, and then adding each thought to the box can be another helpful tool to contain these thoughts and feelings.

→ **Pack:** Once you have packed your thoughts into the "inner obstacles" box, visualize yourself closing the lid and placing the box on the other side of the room. With the box packed up on the other side of the room, you can see the box but it is not in your way. This exercise can help you to see your inner obstacles differently.

Visualization for Thoughts: "Passing Clouds"

Many times, your thoughts come so quickly that it can be challenging to notice them. You may feel flooded with thoughts that can cause emotional reactions. If you found it challenging to notice the thoughts in the above exercise like many of my clients, you may want to start with a visualization. This mindfulness strategy can help you notice your thoughts coming and going.

Close your eyes and imagine you're sitting on a park bench, looking up at the sky; the sun is shining and there are clouds passing by. Imagine each thought is a different cloud; you can see it there in the distance, and then it passes by. Some of the clouds may be helpful, while some are unhelpful inner obstacles. Notice that you feel relaxed while you're watching the clouds pass by, as if you're enjoying watching them at a peaceful park. This visualization is another way to get space from your thoughts, helping them to feel less overwhelming.

Visualizations for Feelings: Feelings as Objects

Mindfulness techniques can also be used to view your emotions more objectively which can help us be less reactive during stressful situations.

At times, your emotions can cause us to feel stuck. We may not always be tuned in to our emotions, sometimes we may notice physical sensations of feeling anxious or feeling sad. Paying attention to the physical sensations related to our emotions can also help to give us space from the emotion and feel less overwhelmed.

The first step in applying mindfulness to feelings is to get curious about what you are feeling physically. For example, whenever I feel sad, I ask myself *where does this show up in my body?* Then I check in with myself and notice that I feel it in my chest. And then, being curious about it, I ask myself *what is it that I'm feeling? Is it a tightness? Is it a heaviness?*

The goal of asking these questions is trying to identify how it looks, how it feels, and creating a visual image of the emotion. For example, I'm feeling sad and the heaviness in my chest feels like a bright red, ten-pound brick.

> **I'm feeling sad and the heaviness in my chest feels like a bright red, ten-pound brick.**

Once I am able to give it a shape, size, and color, then visualize yourself taking it out and imagine holding it in your hand. Notice any difference in how it feels when you're holding the emotion in your hand versus when the emotion is in your body.

Self-Compassion

Growing up, most of us learned the skill of compassion; caring for others and thinking about how they feel. However, you may not have learned to apply these skills to yourself.

Self-compassion, as defined by Dr. Kristin Neff, a pioneer in the field of self-compassion research, is "being warm and understanding toward ourselves when we suffer, fail, or feel inadequate, rather than flagellating ourselves with self-criticism." As a leader, cultivating the skill of self-compassion can foster growth and development, and can help you to stay aligned with your purpose.

In other words, the practice of self-compassion allows you to continue to push forward in the face of failure. It is a tool that can be used to support yourself or as I like to say learning to be your own cheerleader.

If you think about how you treat your friends, chances are that you offer statements of support when they are having a tough time. You may act as their cheerleader when they are feeling discouraged or down. Self-compassion is the practice of talking to yourself the way you would talk to a friend.

Having self-compassion for your thoughts and feelings can help you to accept them and focus on what is in your control. You are in control of whether or not you let your thoughts and feelings keep you from pursuing your goals.

Talking About It: Support from Others

In addition to mindfulness, saying your thoughts aloud and verbally acknowledging your feelings can be a first step in noticing them. Identifying people in your life who are supportive and whom you trust to talk to can also be helpful.

Talking about your thoughts and feelings with others can help you gain perspective and identify distortions. People who you know and trust can be helpful in identifying inaccuracies in your thinking. Revealing your thoughts to others can also normalize your experience, provide support, and make you feel less alone with your thoughts.

Friends and family who are supportive can act as sounding boards for your thoughts. Additionally, you may have supportive colleagues who can actively listen to you. However, friends, family, and colleagues may offer unhelpful advice, or they may not understand what you are experiencing. And, when unhelpful thoughts and feelings are powerful and intense, hearing words of encouragement or that your thoughts aren't accurate may not be enough.

Another option, which can be the most effective place to talk about your thoughts related to self-doubt and fear at work, is with an executive coach. An executive coach can provide a safe and non-judgmental space to explore and challenge your thoughts. In addition to providing an objective perspective, a coach can help you understand how unhelpful thoughts can work against your goals and develop a plan to address these thoughts.

Most people and leaders find themselves stuck or over-thinking from time to time. However, there may be times when being stuck or overthinking becomes a significant problem that affects their functioning at work and in their personal lives. For example, substance abuse may be negatively affecting work performance. In situations like this, coaching can be more harmful than helpful.

When working with a coaching client, I can identify the warning signs that fear or doubt may be signs of a more serious, diagnosable mental health condition. If fear, anxiety, or doubt is causing impairment in daily functioning, then I use my clinical skills to determine if a referral to a licensed mental health provider is warranted. Based on the severity of the symptoms and the mental health provider's recommendation, we may pause coaching until symptoms have improved or continue coaching in parallel with therapy.

How Did Marla Turn It Around?

For Marla, the artist and influencer, watching herself on video is a way to conquer her imposter syndrome feelings. When brushing her teeth in the morning, she watches her own social media videos. She listens to herself and reminds herself that she is communicating her why and being herself.

"I really like what I'm doing. This is the message I want to get across!" This method of self-talk and celebrating wins keeps Marla going when anxious thoughts and feelings creep up. Continuing to take steps toward her goals, even when these thoughts and feelings are present, has enabled Marla to set and reach new goals of expanding her services far beyond selling art.

CHAPTER 4

SQUARE #2: WHAT HAPPENS WHEN INTERNAL OBSTACLES GET IN THE WAY?

> *"There are plenty of difficult obstacles in your path. Don't allow yourself to be one of them."*
> **RALPH MARSTON**

Working twelve-hour shifts with no breaks as a bartender and server, Itzel felt the stress was just too much. She began to experience anxiety and panic attacks that made it hard to work. When she wasn't at work, she was exhausted, and was too tired to focus on self-care.

Itzel had gone to film school and felt stuck in a dead-end job, too far away from her dreams. She had the ambition to create content using her photography skills—but *how*, when it seemed like her own body wasn't cooperating? Intense periods of having a racing heart, rapid breathing, feeling anxiety and thoughts that something was physically wrong with her made it hard to do anything. She experienced an overwhelmingly intense fear that something could be physically wrong with her and she didn't know what to do. But Itzel knew one thing, she wasn't ready to say her working days were over.

Fear was causing Itzel to feel stuck. She wasn't doing any of the things she loved, she was unhappy in her workplace, and she wasn't taking care of herself. Her first step was making the decision to take some time off to figure it out. Next, she went to see a doctor. Although the doctors found no health conditions (aside from panic attacks), her anxiety continued to rule her life. It came to the point where even leaving the house required careful planning because she needed an escape route in case she was hit with a bout of panic. Doctors talked about medication and disability but Itzel was determined to take a more holistic path. She had to find other ways to manage her stress and the path to getting there was through self-awareness.

Through this self-awareness journey, Itzel realized that she wasn't managing her stress. Although it initially seemed like her job was the culprit, it was much more than that. Itzel started to read books and talk to others about what she was experiencing.

She realized that by not doing certain things, she was actually making her stress worse. She didn't have a self-care routine; she wasn't focused on diet, and exercise was not part of her routine. Itzel also noticed that in her personal life, when others would ask for help, she had a hard time saying no. The fear that people wouldn't like her or that they would be upset with her caused her to say yes even though her plate was more than full. This lack of boundaries further limited her time for herself and it was adding an additional layer of stress.

Prioritizing self-care and developing boundaries were key elements of getting back to feeling herself again. She started eating healthy and began incorporating exercise into her routine. And, although it was scary, Itzel started setting boundaries and realized that she felt better and others understood when she decided to say no.

Itzel didn't have a plan in terms of her career path, but she started thinking about what was important—doing what she loved and supporting her community. The hobby she loved, photography and videography, became her focus. Itzel noticed that when she was taking pictures and videos, she wasn't thinking about what was wrong and didn't feel anxious. Her hobby led to her first gig as a wedding photographer. Even though she experienced fear and doubt while embarking on this new path, she was doing what she loved. And, while it began with weddings, she expanded to taking pictures and video content for restaurants and Westchester Blogger was born.

Itzel was able to help and support the community using her hobby, combining her passion with her purpose. Her confidence began to build with each successful business she served. Itzel quickly became the go-to source for restaurant reviews and events in her county. Fifty thousand plus followers later, Itzel has a thriving business that she loves as a social media influencer who promotes local businesses and also trains others on social media marketing to help their businesses grow.

What Happens When Inner Obstacles Get in the Way?

Self-limiting thoughts and feelings can make pursuing your goals feel pointless or impossible. Such internal obstacles can lead to actions that move you in the opposite direction of your goals.

When unhelpful thoughts and feelings show up, they can demotivate you and lead to avoiding doing what's important. Fear, doubt, sadness, anger and related thoughts can cause avoidance, procrastination, and unhealthy coping mechanisms. And, in turn, what you do when unhelpful thoughts and feelings show up can cause you to have more unhelpful thoughts and feelings.

These external behaviors are Square 2 of the 4-Square Model.

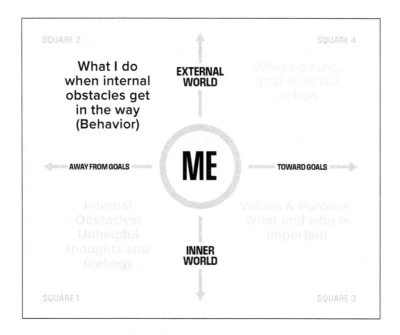

Like Itzel, you may get stuck and fail to do what's important toward furthering your career goals by doing nothing or doing something that doesn't help you.

Instead of taking action and pursuing her passion, Itzel became stuck in a cycle of anxiety that limited her ability to create a path for her future that was aligned with her values. The more she felt unhelpful feelings of anxiety and fear, the more she avoided doing what she loved, and this made her feel even worse. Itzel wasn't taking steps to manage her stress and she wasn't taking steps toward identifying her goals and making a plan to get there.

If you think back about times in your life where you've felt stuck, were there limiting thoughts and feelings getting in your way? Was fear or doubt preventing you from doing what was important? What did you do when you felt stuck? This self-reflection exercise can help you to identify what happens when limiting thoughts and feelings show up.

Stress Gets in the Way

We wear many hats and are often forced to juggle multiple work-related tasks, and still find time for personal priorities. A reoccurring theme for the interviewees was that making time for everything and everyone was an ongoing challenge. Whether it was a business leader, artist, influencer, or DJ, this challenge was one they all experienced.

Focusing on your own needs is necessary to maintain wellness, which can positively impact productivity, creativity, decision-making and empathy. In addition, modeling self-care can influence others in a positive way. However, for me (and for many of my clients), when things became non-stop in my first leadership role, the first thing I cut from my schedule was self-care.

Stress can distract us and even prevent us from focusing on our goals. Stress can come from inner obstacles, outside circumstances, and from our own behaviors. Let's look more closely at what stress is and how it affects us.

What Is Stress?

Stress is a physical response that involves being in a state of worry as a result of situations perceived as a threat. The threat can range from acute life or death situations to chronic, daily pressure. Stress impacts all of the systems of our bodies and can take a physical and mental toll on your health. Stress influences our thoughts and behaviors. And, stress can be amplified by your unhelpful thoughts, feelings, and behaviors. While we need some level of stress to stay motivated and get things done, keeping stress at a manageable level is a constant, necessary battle to avoid burnout.

Why Do I Have Stress?

Stress is the body's response to chronic pressure or reactive circumstances. Initially, in the days of the cave man, we responded to stressors by reacting with a "fight, flight, or freeze" response, and after the threat was over, our body returned to a normal state. In our modern world, the chronic pressure and demands of work, relationships, and finances have a long-term impact on us physically and emotionally—the stressors don't go away and we can remain in a chronic state of reactivity and stress.

How Does Stress Impact Me?

In perceived life-threatening situations, the body is kicked into what is often called fight or flight, or survival mode: adrenaline and cortisol increase, digestion shuts down, heart rate and blood pressure increase, and you experience heightened alertness. You become physically primed to survive the situation and fight the tiger or run away.

However, while this survival mechanism was essential in the primitive days for responding to danger, in current times, we are much less frequently faced with the same level of physical danger. When we perceive a threat, our body is still primed for survival. And, when the threat does not subside, our body remains in this heightened mode which can lead to chronic stress resulting in physical and emotional symptoms including headaches, muscle pain, gastric issues, changes in sleep patterns, and feelings of irritability, sadness, and anxiety. Further, chronic stress can lead to a variety of health and mental health-related conditions and diagnoses.

Stress can cause you to put off self-care and engage in unhealthy coping mechanisms. During times of stress, you may be more likely to use substances, make poor diet choices, and not get enough sleep. And, when you are under stress, you may be less likely to acknowledge positive events and focus on taking steps toward your goals.

How Does Stress Impact Me Professionally?

The most detrimental impact of chronic stress when it comes to work is *burnout*. Burnout occurs when you feel mentally and physically exhausted, productivity decreases, and you begin to feel cynical about work. "In 2019, the World Health Organization classified burnout as an occupational phenomenon 'resulting from chronic workplace stress that has not been successfully managed.'"[8]
Burnout can lead to physical and mental health challenges, and in worst-case scenarios may impair you to the point where you can no longer work.

Because stress impacts both mood and physical health, it can negatively impact you at work in a variety of ways including strained relationships or conflict with colleagues and customers due to increased irritability, poor decision-making, decreased productivity, poor concentration, decreased creativity, and trouble prioritizing tasks.

Early on in my career, I failed at managing my stress. Because I felt like I had so much to learn and get done, I started working

8 American Heart Association News. "How Job Burnout Can Hurt Your Health – and What to Do about It." October 12, 2022. https://www.heart.org/en/news/2022/10/12/how-job-burnout-can-hurt-your-health-and-what-to-do-about-it.

longer hours and skipping important self-care priorities like going to the gym. I wasn't focused on all that was important.

While my mindset was that I had to work harder and longer to be successful, I learned the hard way that this was not the path to success, but rather the path to illness. The extra time and energy I spent spinning my wheels without the guidance, support, or tools to create a clear path for success and growth was futile. Not having a clear focus combined with failing to prioritize self-care caused my stress levels to skyrocket. After a year of high stress, I developed a virus that completely took me down. Unable to work and too ill to complete many daily activities, my grind came to a complete halt.

> ## This was not the path to success, but rather the path to illness.

The strategies that helped me to recover from illness and disability continue to guide me today. Self-awareness was the first step in recovery from stress and changing the stressful environment. I came to the conclusion after self-reflection and therapy that my current work environment did not provide a clear strategy to help me grow or thrive. In addition, the organizational values did not align with my own values. I realized that self-care trumped work and without it, I would not be able to work again.

Once my self-awareness grew, my focus became managing my stress, which shifted from workplace issues to health concerns. I decided to change everything. I started prioritizing self-care and I took a job that aligned with what was important to me—helping students to manage stress and incorporate self-care as part of their routine. I made a cross country move which I had wanted to do for many years. And interestingly, I ended up teaching a graduate course on stress management at a local college where I had received my undergraduate degree.

Stress and the 4-Square Model

Developing self-awareness of your thoughts and behaviors can help you determine your sources of stress. If you look at the two left squares, your stress can be coming from unhelpful thoughts, feelings and related behaviors.

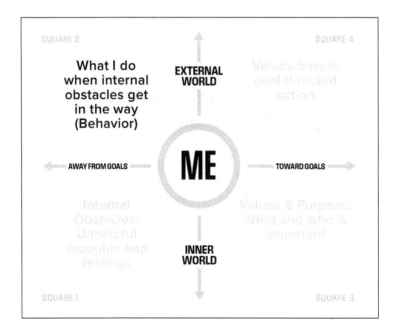

The big takeaway—if your thoughts and feelings are limiting you, then your behaviors are not fully aligned with your goals and purpose. Behaviors that take you away from your goals (including everything from avoiding taking steps toward your goals to using substances to avoid unhelpful feelings) often *cause* stress. In addition, not focusing on your values and goals (the right two squares) can cause stress.

Similarly, being unaware of Square 3 (your values and purpose), and not living in alignment with your values and purpose, can cause stress (e.g., having a job that you're not passionate about). Lastly, when considering who and what is important to you in Square 3, a major source of stress can come from excluding *yourself* from the list of *who* is important to you. For example, despite Itzel's ambitions, she was so stressed that her self-care got put on the back burner, causing health issues that kept her from pursuing her dreams.

Psychology-Based Self-Awareness Strategies to Overcome Inner Obstacles

Developing self-awareness regarding the importance of self-care, breaks, boundaries, and support are strategies to help maximize your growth.

- ➜ Self-Reflection Stress Check
- ➜ Self-care Necessities
- ➜ Social Support

- Boundary Management
- Situational Zoom Out

Self-Reflection Stress Check

Bringing your awareness to thoughts, feelings, and situations in which you feel stressed is key to understanding how you and your environment impact your stress level.

- What do you feel, physically, when you're under stress?
- What thoughts and emotions come up for you that cause stress?
- Refer back to Square 1 (from Chapter 3) to identify thoughts and feelings that get in the way with your own stress response. Then ask yourself:
  - What are you typically doing when you feel stressed?
  - What situations cause you stress?
  - Do you feel this way most of the time or just in specific situations?
- Make a list of situations and tasks that cause you to feel stressed.
  - Are there changes you can make to your environment to reduce stress? After you have given this some thought, you are ready to look at what strategies you are already implementing and where you might make changes.

Self-care Necessities: Sleep, Physical activity, Nutrition, Mindfulness

Many of those with influence find that having a multitude of tasks and priorities causes them to neglect self-care. Unfortunately, self-care tends to be pushed to the end of the list, going unprioritized. From my experience, when self-care got pushed to the bottom of the list, it took illness to force me to make changes and reprioritize self-care.

Basic self-care (sleep, nutrition, physical and emotional wellness strategies) impacts how we respond to stress and can prevent illness and burnout. But ironically, stress can sometimes cause us to ignore self-care. Proactively focusing on getting enough sleep, the right nutrition, consistent physical activity, taking breaks, and engaging in enjoyable activities can buffer against stress. And, developing these habits proactively and prioritizing them can make it easier to keep them going during stressful times.

Mindfulness includes any activity where you are fully present and engaging all of your senses. Your mind is focused on what you're doing in the present moment, not in the past or the future. For some, this may be meditation but it can also be engaging in a new, enjoyable, or even mundane activity. Marla, the artist, practices mindfulness when she creates her paintings. She immerses herself in the process and is fully focused on creating. You can even practice mindfulness when brushing your teeth by attending to the taste of the toothpaste, the smell of the toothpaste, and the feeling of the toothbrush on your teeth.

Social Support: Personal Board of Directors, Mastermind Groups, and Mentorship

I often hear leaders, business owners, and influencers express feelings of loneliness. Without the right support, it can be harder to stay motivated and keep going. Not talking about your challenges can increase anxious thoughts and feelings, allowing them to become more powerful and more likely to derail you from your goals. Social support is essential for wellbeing, decision-making, and overall effectiveness.

Support from family, friends, and community can mitigate stress and provide a source of accountability. In addition to providing emotional support, having others to talk to can provide different perspectives and insights as well as help with problem-solving. Proactively seeking support can also provide an outlet for stress and can help make the burden of an ongoing to-do list along with stressful events less overwhelming.

"Research by the Centers for Disease Control and Prevention shows that strong social bonds can protect against stress-related physical and mental illnesses like heart disease and depression, cutting your risk of early death by 50%. But recruiting that support can be easier said than done. In this year's Stress in America survey, two-thirds of adults said they could've used more emotional support in the past year, and over half wished they had someone to turn to for advice."[9]

---

9 Medaris, Anna. 2023. "6 Things Researchers Want You to Know About Stress." American Psychological Association (APA). November 1, 2023. https://www.apa.org/topics/stress/research-findings.

This quote emphasizes the importance of social support as well as how common it is for people to lack adequate support. Finding social support usually takes effort. Depending on what you need support regarding, you may want to ask different people for different types of support. Or you may only have one go-to person for support.

Asking for support and being specific in what type of support you ask for has been a helpful strategy for me, the clients I work with, and those I interviewed for this book. For example, rather than saying to someone, "I need support," I might say, "Can you listen to me talk through a challenging situation with a colleague for 10 minutes?" I find that being this specific can help others understand how best to support you and increase your ability to get the support you need.

And, just like a company has a board of directors that helps guide the company with their wisdom and experience so that the company can be the most successful, a personal board of directors is a group of people that you pull together, a super squad that shares their unique perspectives, experience, and skills to help guide you toward the life that you envision for yourself.

Support for a Trend-Setting Influencer

Therese, a psychologist and digital nomad, realized that the power of influence comes from within but it actually took having support to make this realization. She used three strategies to develop her support network, by creating:

1. Her own personal board of directors.
2. A mastermind group with other like-minded colleagues.
3. Support from mentors.

Each of these strategies offered a different type of support that has had unique benefits. Having support helped Therese to reach her goals, level up her influence, and grow personally and professionally.

When Therese brought together her board of directors, she chose different people who she admired something about or had a life purpose that was aligned with hers. She chose a psychologist who was a mother of four, and a pastor at a church who she considered to be an amazing leader. Therese sought out people who were further down the road than she was—people who represented different parts of her dream. Having their leadership and guidance over the years has really helped her.

Once she assembled her board, she began sending them an email once a month saying, "Here's what's going on. Here are my problem areas. Here's where I need help and support." Following this prompt, they share whatever wisdom or insight they have or just keep her in their thoughts. Having this support helped Therese to be intentional and strategic about her direction.

At the same time, as Therese wanted to start a virtual therapy practice (years before the pandemic when this was unheard of), she received negative feedback from other psychologists who said it would never work and that she wouldn't be successful. Instead of letting this feedback sway her from pursuing her goal, she sought out other forward-thinking psychologists. She created a mastermind group of other psychologists who shared a similar goal. They met regularly and shared their experiences with moving into a business that had never before been virtual. This group was a great source of support for Therese on her journey that at one point had felt lonely.

Lastly, from the time Therese was a college student, she was moved by the impact of mentorship. After working for AmeriCorps running an after-school program that provided mentors to kids and at risk schools, she realized the power of mentorship to change lives by guiding others and letting them know what's possible. The powerful experience of being a mentor caused her to realize that she needed her own mentor. At each stage of her life, mentors have helped her by sharing their own experiences. Therese described the power of having mentors as "going on a path on a trip and you've never been on that trip before but there's other people that have and they can say, 'When you get here, make sure you turn this corner and see this or don't miss that when you go that way.' Invaluable insight!"

Boundary Management

"Boundaries are the mental, emotional, and physical limits people maintain with respect to others and their environment, and psychologists consider them healthy if they ensure an individual's continued well-being and stability. They serve many valuable functions. They help protect us, clarify our own responsibilities and those of others, and preserve our physical and emotional energy. They help us stay focused on ourselves, honor our values and standards, and identify our personal limits."[10]

Boundaries regarding how to separate work and personal life can be a challenge for many leaders. Purpose-driven

---

10 Gionta, Dana, and Liz Sweigart. 2022. "How Healthy Boundaries Build Trust in the Workplace." Strategy+Business. February 15, 2022. https://www.strategy-business.com/article/How-healthy-boundaries-build-trust-in-the-workplace.

leaders, business owners, and influencers love the work they do and because of this, it can be easy for work and personal life to overlap. In addition, a desire to help others can lead to putting others first at the expense of your personal time and priorities.

Boundaries regarding breaks is key for success, effectiveness, and wellbeing. Taking breaks throughout the work day as well as taking time off from work are equally important. Proactively scheduling breaks during the day to include time for meals and time away from screens can help to manage stress and maintain productivity.

The three steps to better boundary management according to psychologists Gionta and Sweigart are: identifying boundaries, setting boundaries,[11] and maintaining boundaries. Self-reflection about your behaviors in relationships can be the first step to identifying if you may benefit from setting more boundaries.

Common indicators that you may not have effective boundaries are difficulty saying "no," overcommitting to responsibilities, and neglecting self-care. If you find yourself in these situations, reviewing your values can help you determine what changes you'd like to make. Then, the next step is communicating those boundaries assertively.

11 ibid

Situational Zoom Out

A visualization strategy that can help to see the situation clearly when emotions are running high is zooming out from the situation. By this, I mean picture yourself in the situation that's causing an emotional response on the sidewalk in a city. Then, imagine you take a glass elevator up to the roof of a building. As you're standing in the elevator, you can see yourself in the situation down below, but as you go up, floor by floor, you are removing yourself from the emotionally charged situation. It's not a long ride to the top, but when you arrive, the elevator doors open, and you walk out onto the rooftop toward the railing, where you look down and see yourself below. Once you have this view of your situation, ask yourself the following questions:

- What do you see yourself doing?
- How does your new view from above change the situation?
- How do you feel about what you see from this view?
- How do you see yourself handling the situation?
- Are you handling the situation in a way that feels good to you?
- If not, what might you do differently?

Taking this view of the situation and asking yourself these questions can help you gain needed distance from your internal experience and emotions (Square 1), and allow you to view your behaviors (Square 2) more objectively.

How Did Itzel Turn It Around?

When Itzel made the commitment to prioritize her self-care, she began a years-long journey to overcome her stress-related health issues. Along the way, she practiced such strategies as seeking support, and boundary-setting.

As her career as an influencer took off, she doubled-down on her self-care and support. Setting boundaries professionally, in particular, was important for her to overcome challenging times.

Early on when she started Westchester Blogger, she said yes to everything because she had a fear of letting clients down. This led to feeling overwhelmed and stressed. Although it was hard to learn to say no, Itzel found that being honest helps and her clients have been very understanding.

Today, Itzel has helped countless business owners and influencers grow their audience, promote their business, and develop their brand. Her anxiety no longer gets in the way because she is doing what she loves and she "trusts the process."

CHAPTER 5

SQUARE #3: VALUES AND PURPOSE

> *"When your values are clear to you, making decisions becomes easier."*
> **ROY E. DISNEY**

Dr. Therese Mascardo is a clinical psychologist and digital nomad. For years, she's been a trailblazer by having a *virtual* private practice. Even before the pandemic, at a time when most clinicians agreed that meeting with clients over Zoom couldn't be done, she went virtual. At the same time, because of her prior career in marketing in the luxury brand industry, she used this knowledge to level up her influence; developing her own business, building a social media following of over 26,000, and releasing a workbook to help others live a life they love. And she does so in Lisbon,

Portugal, where she moved in 2019 to create the life that she had always wanted.

Therese's influence is clear; she is a purpose-driven leader and inspiration to me and many others. She is vulnerable and authentic and openly speaks of her failures, struggles, and life experiences. I chose to interview her for all of these reasons.

I was curious about her ability to create a remote practice when other psychologists thought it couldn't be done. (As a psychologist during the pre-pandemic years, I never even entertained the possibility that my work could be done virtually.) I was equally impressed by her ability to move to another country where she didn't know anyone or know the language. Most of all, I wondered—*Did a greater purpose drive her, and how did she overcome obstacles along the way? How did her why shift over time?*

> "Today, my 'why' is about helping people thrive and live life to the very fullest and to overcome any obstacles that get in the way of them living a life where they can truly feel like the joy and the excitement and the adventure of life."
>
> "If you know me and my story, I lost my brother in 2009 to suicide and that was already when I was a therapist. So that was a very profound, jarring moment in life. Seeing someone that was so close to me that was so disconnected from wanting to live—the event shocked me and made me want to explore how I could help other people to not feel

that way and to not go through the loss of losing someone in that same way. That extraordinarily painful experience actually focused me in on my why: *I'm here because I want people to thrive. I want people to do everything that they can so that they can feel happiness and joy in this lifetime. And even if they can't, then to find a way through it."*

"Learning my 'why' has been a lifelong process that continues to get refined every day. But one of the things that's guided me along the way is learning about myself. So that's been through different things like taking personality tests when I was 16 online, and that would be like the Myers Briggs and the Enneagram. And just learning about the kind of the things that make me unique, and maybe the things that I'm naturally good at. I'm also really into the StrengthsFinder. I mean, like, if there's a personality test, I'm into it, right. And then when I was in college, trying to kind of figure out my 'why,' I considered being a doctor—but, my gosh, the sight of blood makes me queasy, so this is probably not a good idea. But I'd been so conditioned by my Filipino parents: 'You will be a doctor.'"

Learning my 'why' has been a lifelong process that continues to get refined every day.

"Then when I was a sophomore at UC Berkeley, I took my first Psych 101 class, as part of the requirements for my other major, which was mass communications. And when I took Psych 101, I realized that there was this whole new world that kind of opened up to me, and that there was an entire field devoted to people and I had always really loved people. So knowing that that was kind of like, the guide for me as I progressed through life and became a psychologist."

"I'm going to be 41 this week, and looking back, I can see all these little threads that have contributed to the entire picture of my life today—but of course we can't always see these threads in the moment."

"When I was 12, I volunteered at a hospital, where I learned about people who are ill and how to care for them.

- I worked in hospitality and I used to do events for 1000s of people
- I worked at a church
- I worked for a food tourism company in Los Angeles
- I studied mass communications in college.
- I became a doctor in psychology.

"Perhaps at the time, all these things seemed super random and disconnected. But now, in hindsight, they all kind of make sense because they all fit into this picture of living life to the fullest."

"What I do today—and what I've always done—is about people. It's about hospitality. It's about enjoying life. It's about the senses. It's about psychology. Right? It's actually kind of funny to see the through line, which you can only see when you're looking back."

Lastly, Therese emphasizes the importance of living without regret. "I think this happens for a lot of people: when you lose someone, your priorities shift, your values change. For me that meant I never wanted to have regret. If I have an opportunity to have fun or joy, I'm going to take it, even if I don't see the big picture or have everything figured out. Because I don't want to look back on my life 5, 10, or 15 years from now and regret not doing the wild thing that I had the opportunity to do."

Throughout the years, Therese's *why* statement has continued to change; her why statement has been flexible and expressed in different career paths and life choices. However, a key to her success has been her ability to remain connected to her purpose and values and ride the waves as they have shifted over time.

Purpose and Influence

Finding, understanding, and refining your purpose or the "why" behind why you do the work that you do is an important step to maintaining alignment between your purpose and your actions. Your *why* is your purpose, and underlying your purpose are your values.

Square 3 of the 4-Square Model is comprised of *what matters most to you*. It includes what is important to you, who is important to you, and your purpose. This includes your *values* and is the other side of your inner world, the side that helps you to pursue your goals.

→ Who is important to you?
→ How are you important?
→ What is important to you?
→ What is your purpose?

When listing the answers to these questions in Square 3, sometimes it may be easy to forget to list yourself under the list of people that are important. When you pursue your goals to the exclusion of your own need for self-care, the risk of burnout rises. Making sure you are on the list of who's important can act as a reminder of the importance of setting goals related to self-care.

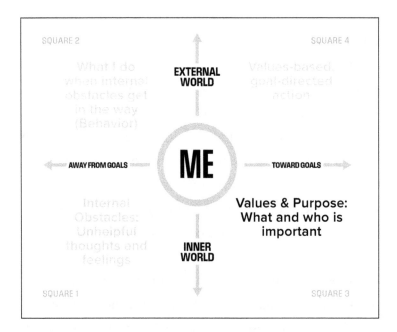

Author Simon Sinek talks about the importance of starting with why when beginning a career or business journey.[12] Having a clear sense of your purpose can help you:

- Identify your goals
- Motivate you
- Enhance your decision making
- Improve your well-being
- Build resilience

Your why lays the foundation for your career or business trajectory while maintaining a balance between work and personal life. Returning to this foundation during difficult

---

12 Sinek, Simon. 2009. *Start With Why: How Great Leaders Inspire Everyone to Take Action.* http://ci.nii.ac.jp/ncid/BB07258461.

or uncertain times can help you to recenter and recommit to your purpose.

Like Therese, people who understand their purpose and are considered by others to be "purpose-driven," often have influence and act as role models to others.

Your why is your purpose and acts as a guide to where you want to go in life. It's your overall mission. Asking yourself the question, "what am I meant to do in life?" often reveals your purpose. It is a broad, long-term goal such as, "I want to help people." Your purpose provides direction and meaning to your life.

People who understand their purpose and act toward it are likely to experience a sense of fulfillment and inspire others to fulfill their purpose. For Therese, her purpose was clear: help people live a life they don't need a vacation from. And for many of us, significant life experiences bring our purpose to the front of our minds. Therese experienced a heightened sense of purpose after losing her brother.

Your Purpose

Are you clear and specific about your purpose? Once you define your purpose, your definition can help you understand and identify your motivation, strengths, and what you enjoy doing.

For example, my purpose from an early age was helping people. While this very broad *why* has remained my mission throughout my career, I have expressed it in a variety of ways, including working in various settings with people of all ages, then moving to helping people to be successful in business and their career, to now including DJs among the many groups of people I help to succeed at work.

Therese is driven by her purpose of helping people live their best lives. Having lost her brother when he was a young adult, him not being able to fulfill his dreams solidified her mission of helping others realize their dreams. For Therese, she leads by example, having made her ultimate dream a reality by starting her dream life in another country where the culture was more in line with her values. In addition, she created a thriving virtual practice and products to help other therapists reach their goals and live a life they don't need a vacation from—even recently publishing a workbook to help everyone focus on living their dream life. Her influence has spread globally, and she has helped people from all walks of life to find joy and fulfillment in their lives.

Shirley, a nonprofit founder, began her journey to founding Latino U College Access, after combining her value of education with a need that she saw for guidance with the college process in the Latino community. Although her day job was in advertising, she volunteered at various nonprofits that aligned with her value of giving back to the community where she lived. Years later, her nonprofit, LUCA, has helped hundreds of Latino students successfully get into college—and the organization continues to grow. Shirley was awarded the AARP Purpose Prize for the impact that her purpose-driven organization has had on the students they serve.

Marla, an artist who describes her art as "happy art" and her painting style as abstract expressionism, is driven by her purpose to spread happiness to the world. Her hobby (and love) of painting turned into a profession when she realized the impact that her art was having on others. She was able to influence their emotions in a positive way and wanted to expand her influence to others. She's done this through social media, supporting causes that she cares about with her art, and founding an income-producing business. Today, Marla runs *Marla Beth Designs*, which offers services to other artists and small business owners, alongside her art studio where she offers classes, pop-ups, and hosts events that support the community.

Values and Influence

While your purpose is rooted in your values or what matters most to you, your values are principles of behavior or standards that guide your decision-making and priorities.

People who live according to their values consistently make decisions based on these values and are not swayed or influenced by unhelpful thoughts and feelings. As a result, they become viewed by others as reliable, credible, and trustworthy, and this increases their influence. Self-awareness of your underlying values and staying connected to these values helps to guide your decisions, no matter how stressful the situation may be.

However, for many of us, although our values may be guiding our behavior at times, our awareness of our specific values may not always be top of mind. And, our awareness of how our values connect to our behaviors may be inconsistent or limited.

Purpose-driven people who are often influencers and leaders strive to align and inspire people around a shared purpose. Values are the foundation that drives purpose-driven leaders. Their purpose and values serve as a compass for decision-making and their approach to leadership and career path.

But being purpose-driven is a continual journey that often changes shape over time. An essential component of this journey is developing self-awareness and personal growth and development. This process often entails connecting with and reassessing your values, identifying strengths and areas for development, and goal-setting.

> **Being purpose-driven is a continual journey that often changes shape over time.**

Psychology-based Self-Awareness Strategies for Values and Purpose

Values have a dual impact because they extend beyond yourself to others. If you are acting toward your values, others can see it. They know what you stand for because they see you living it. This increases trust and credibility and can inspire others. That's influence!

When was the last time you thought about your values? What are they? What is important? Who is important? Are your behaviors in alignment with your actions? How do your values impact your influence? The question of "Who and what is important to you?" is a great starting point to increase your awareness of values that are important to you. Here are a few strategies:

- → Values Assessment: What Are Your Values?
- → What Went Well
- → When I'm Gone

Values Assessment: What Are Your Values?

Your values are your judgment of what's important in life. They may or may not be something that you think about on a daily basis. However, assessing and reassessing your values can help you identify your goals—what to keep doing and what to do less of.

Conducting a values assessment is a great way to increase self-awareness and target areas for growth. Steps for values assessment:

- → Reflection
- → Ask yourself questions (what will matter when you're gone – epitaph exercise, what do you enjoy doing, what are you good at, what do you want to learn)
- → Rank your values (values checklist)

What Went Well

The exercise of "What Went Well" was developed by the father of Positive Psychology, Martin Seligman. He found that this exercise helped him to acknowledge positive events that he wasn't paying attention to and led to feeling more positive and focusing less on negative events (even though they still occurred).

I have also found completing this exercise leads to increased self-awareness of positive events, feeling more positive and an increased sense of gratitude. And, every client that completes this exercise also reports positive feelings. In addition, keeping track of what went well can increase your awareness of the things you enjoy which can help to uncover your values.

The "What Went Well" exercise should be completed on a daily basis for two weeks. However, many clients often keep completing this exercise and incorporate it into their daily routine because they find it sparks positive feelings that increase motivation.

Here are the steps for completing "What Went Well":

→ At the end of each day (for a two-week period), write down (on paper or in your phone) three things that went well.

→ Things that "went well" can be big or small, they can be things you did or experienced that sparked positive feelings such as happiness, calm or enjoyment. For example, you took a break during the work day and sat on a bench outside for five minutes, or you spoke to a close friend on the phone.

→ If there are days you struggle to identify three positive things, that's ok and is common. But don't give up. Challenging yourself to identify three things, no matter how small. If you can only come up with two, that's ok too. You may find the next day you're more conscious of making an effort to participate in enjoyable activities.

→ After the two-week period, look back on your list and ask yourself how does it feel when you read the list?

How did this exercise change your awareness? What do you want to do more of?

When I'm Gone

This self-reflection exercise is designed to get you in touch with your values and purpose at a deeper level. While some may find this exercise challenging or anxiety-inducing because it requires you to visualize your memorial service, I encourage you to try it despite any difficult thoughts and feelings that may arise. You will need about ten minutes to complete this exercise. If you do notice inner obstacles coming to the surface, acknowledge them, and return to the exercise instructions.

- Find a comfortable space and limit distractions.
- Close your eyes and take a few deep breaths to ground yourself.
- *Imagine you are attending your own memorial service. Who's there? What does the room look like? Listen to the people who come up to speak about you. What words do they use to describe you, what stories do they tell, what are their emotions? What are people saying about you? How do they describe your life, actions, influence, and impact?*
- After you have answered these questions, slowly bring yourself back to the present moment.
- Then write down the answers to these questions: What would you want people to say about you at your memorial? How do you want to be remembered? Try

to be as specific and detailed as possible and consider different areas of your life, such as professional accomplishments, personal growth, and the relationships with those close to you and your community.

→ Then answer the following questions: How do your answers align with your current life and actions? What changes might you make to improve this alignment?

This exercise can help clarify your sense of purpose and core values, providing guidance for meaningful goal-setting which we will dive into next.

Values and Purpose: My Story

Through the years, my *why* continued to shift over time and so has my influence. My influence is no longer limited to students and clients, I'm having a positive influence on countless workplaces and leaders, my community and many people who I don't even know personally.

A transformative experience back in 2015 was the spark that would lead to a brightly burning fire years later. I attended my first Electronic Dance Music (EDM) festival having no idea that it would have such a major and lasting impact. I knew two songs in this genre and decided to give it a try. I didn't realize that there was a whole culture behind the music and a scene that drew me in immediately.

I had the misconception that ravers liked drugs and music with no words. That festival in Puerto Rico exposed me to a new world that was not about drugs—it was about community, connection, inclusivity, and kindness. It was about PLUR— peace, love, unity, and respect.

The feeling that I felt when surrounded by thousands of other people who shared these values and loved the music was unlike any other concert or show I had ever experienced. After two days of experiencing a world that felt in stark contrast to the real world, I felt part of something bigger and a sense of common humanity. I had found a new passion in EDM music and its community.

Attending festivals became a reason to travel and a great way to meet new people who shared similar values. Exploring the different subgenres within EDM and going to see different DJs play was fascinating and became my go-to pastime when I wasn't working. Engaging with this community and getting to know DJs and other people in the industry helped me to understand their struggles and what it takes to be successful from a psychology standpoint. I saw many parallels between the business world and the DJ world and I also realized that DJs didn't always know the psychology behind being successful.

My next step was merging my passion for EDM and for helping others be successful to help DJs use psychology-based strategies to overcome the many challenges of becoming a successful DJ.

Today, I would describe myself as purpose-driven and passion-driven in a different way than when I first embarked on the journey to becoming a psychologist. I have a clear sense of my "why" and a vision that is aimed at making a positive difference in the world.

CHAPTER 6

SQUARE #4: VALUES-BASED, GOAL-DIRECTED ACTION

> "Stay focused, go after your dreams, and keep moving toward your goals."
> **LL COOL J**

After years working in Hispanic marketing and advertising, Shirley decided that although she enjoyed her work, she wanted to help her community in a different and more life-changing way. She forged a new career path in the nonprofit world and pursued a master's degree in nonprofit management. Through her nonprofit work and her life experience as a first-generation college student, she founded a nonprofit to help high school students called Latino U College Access (LUCA).

Shirley was highly motivated to fulfill LUCA's mission to help first generation Latino college students navigate the college application process and succeed in getting a college degree. Her strong drive and sense of purpose led to working long hours. The demands of starting a nonprofit with a small team were intense.

Shirley was applying her knowledge from working in nonprofits along with what she learned in her coursework, but she had never founded a nonprofit. She spent countless hours preparing for presentations and learning how to build a successful nonprofit. The demand of running a nonprofit combined with her extreme enthusiasm and dedication led her to work long hours and neglect self-care such as taking breaks and making time for exercise.

Shirley was doing what was important—focusing on building LUCA—but she wasn't doing *all* that was important. Her focus on work took a toll personally, causing her to miss family dinners.

After several years of intense work and building her team, Shirley recognized the need for a better work-life balance. With the support of her family, she made the difficult decision to change her role at LUCA. Her new role has allowed her to focus on all of the things that are important to her at work and personally.

Shirley recognized after years of focusing on building the business and the students she served, that her life was unbalanced when it came to the things she valued. She wasn't making time for herself and she wasn't spending the amount of time with her family that she wanted to. The business had grown and Shirley had a reliable team that supported LUCA's mission and it was time to shift her role in the organization.

Shirley decided to change her role to achieve more balance in her life. Her self-awareness, continuous learning mindset, and willingness to ask for help all facilitated the shift away from being the sole leader of LUCA. Although it was difficult to step back from a role that was so rewarding, she found it equally rewarding to build a leadership team, still have a part in LUCA, and get time to focus on all that mattered to her both professionally and personally.

Values-Based, Goal-Directed Action

Square 4 of the 4-Square Model is your behavior—what other people can see that you're doing. It's your behaviors and actions that are guided by your purpose and values. It's "how" you show who and what matters along with your purpose to the world (Square 3). These behaviors are guided by your purpose and values and are likely tied to your goals.

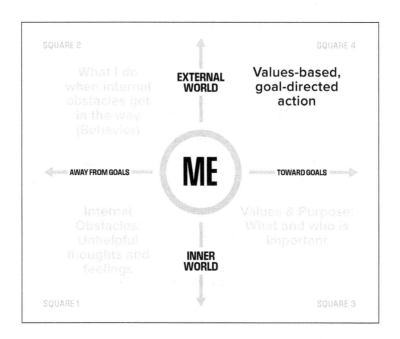

When you act toward your values, what are you doing? How can people see what matters to you? For example, if you care about making music, the outside world may see you spending time in the studio or taking a music production class. This is your values in action. Now that you have completed your values assessment, ask yourself what am I doing or what could I be doing that others can see toward my values?

When your values guide your behaviors, you will experience an increased sense of fulfillment when you are engaging in these actions. And, increased self-awareness regarding connecting your values and purpose to your behaviors naturally levels up your influence. You must look within for values, but it's the outside world that can see them in action.

> **You must look within for values, but it's the outside world that can see them in action.**

This 4th square is a list of purpose-based actions and indicates what you are doing or want to be doing to reach your goals. Your values and purpose can act as a guide to decision-making related to behaviors you list in this square. Square 3 (Values and Purpose) and Square 4 (Values-Based, Goal-Directed Action) comprise your aspirations and goal-directed behaviors.

Increasing your awareness of your behaviors (Square 4) that align with your values and purpose is a step toward consistently being the person you want to be. When you engage in behaviors that are aligned with your values and purpose, your influence grows and you are more likely to be viewed as a leader.

Connecting Values to Goals

Your values can guide the development of your goals. Values-based behaviors move you in the direction of your goals and clearly identifying goals will allow you to develop a plan with action steps, track progress, boost motivation, and hold yourself accountable. In addition, tracking progress and accomplishments can increase confidence and help with decision-making.

Professional and personal values-based goals contribute to a fulfilling life. When your goals are aligned with your personal values, they have more meaning and this can increase motivation and enjoyment when taking actions toward them. In addition, your influence increases and you become a role model to others when your words match your behaviors.

Psychology-based Self-Awareness Strategies to Unlock Your Inner Leader

Self-awareness strategies can help you develop emotional intelligence, manage stress, make better decisions, build resilience, and improve communication, all of which can make you a more authentic and confident leader. With improved self-awareness related to values and behaviors comes an increased alignment between what you say and what you do, thereby increasing your credibility and influence.

The following exercises are designed to increase your alignment between your values and behaviors, and increase your commitment to values-based actions.

- ➦ Self-reflection
- ➦ Aligned Goal-Setting
- ➦ Celebrating Small Wins
- ➦ Self-Talk

Self-Reflection

Reflecting on your daily routine and keeping a log of existing behaviors that align with your values and purpose can help you to list these behaviors in Square 4. This exercise can help you bridge the gap between your values that may be abstract and your concrete actions.

At the end of the day, spend 10 minutes on journaling your observations. After two weeks, reviewing your entries can help you gain clarity regarding your current behaviors that are aligned with your values. If you find that you struggled to identify values-aligned behaviors in your daily routine, don't be discouraged—this information can still be useful.

Through the exercise, you may find that there are behaviors that you're engaging in that aren't actually related to your goals and values. If this is the case, try visualizing what it might look like to act toward your values. If you're having trouble with this visualization, it can be helpful to think about someone you consider to be a role model and ask yourself what actions do they take that cause you to look up to them. This can help you to generate a list of actions that can become the basis for values-based goals.

Aligned Goal-Setting

With your values and purpose in mind, setting goals that are aligned with your values and purpose can be very motivating because it feels rewarding when you act toward your values.

SMART goals, a commonly accepted framework for setting goals can help you establish goals that you are more likely to accomplish. SMART goals are Specific, Measurable, Achievable, Relevant, and Time-bound. Making your goals specific and measurable is essential for tracking your progress and determining success. Specific goals are not ambiguous, they outline the exact action steps that you need to complete to be successful.

In order to measure progress, having realistic goals with specific actions steps is necessary. Otherwise, it can be hard to identify progress and you may find that you gloss over it. Your goals should be relevant to your values and purpose—if they aren't related to what matters to you, then it won't be worth it.

SMART goals will provide a specific roadmap for success that when guided by your purpose and values will also be motivating. Lastly, setting time deadlines on your goals can also motivate you to reach them in a certain amount of time. Without a deadline, there is no pressure to get it done and you may be more likely to procrastinate and not accomplish the goal.

Here's an example of a SMART goal that I developed when starting *Shaping Success*, my executive coaching and consulting practice:

- → **Specific**: Launch a business consulting practice focusing on small to medium-sized startups.
- → **Measurable**: Secure five paying clients and generate $30,000 in revenue.
- → **Achievable**: Develop my network and expertise in executive coaching and the tech industry to attract initial clients.
- → **Relevant**: Aligns with my purpose for starting the practice—helping people be successful in leadership and in their organization. Align with my values of independence and balance—becoming an independent consultant and helping business leaders find balance using my expertise in psychology.
- → **Time-bound**: Accomplish these objectives within the first six months of launching the practice.

This goal provides a clear definition of success, measurable outcomes, and a set timeframe, while ensuring it's achievable and relevant to my values and purpose starting a consulting practice. Additionally, this goal was aligned with something I cared deeply about - helping leaders and business owners be successful. Having this specific goal with measurable action steps allowed me to track and celebrate my progress and adjust accordingly.

Celebrate Small Wins

Small wins are often the result of actions we're taking toward our values, purpose, and goals. Acknowledging and celebrating these small wins is a strategy that has helped me and has been instrumental for my clients and many of the leaders and influencers whom I interviewed. Common responses to this suggestion are: "That's silly," "It's not a big deal," and "Who cares? It's such a small thing." But those responses fly in the face of truth, which is this—celebrating small wins can help you notice and acknowledge your progress while staying motivated to keep moving forward.

That being said, our brains are wired to attend to threats, which causes us to pay attention to (and sometimes over attend to) negative events. That means positive events are easily pushed to the side and often overlooked or forgotten. By keeping track of small wins, we increase our awareness of progress and allow us time to feel the positive emotions associated with those wins. This exercise can be motivating while also reinforcing small steps toward your larger goals.

Marla, the artist, is a firm believer in celebrating small wins and milestones when it comes to all aspects of her business, not just creating art. No milestone is too small to celebrate and they all add up. She celebrates each step toward larger goals and also reminds herself that she is selling art which is a hard thing to do.

Self-Talk

Using self-talk can help you stay motivated while taking action toward your goals, especially when they may be life-long, purpose-related goals. Talking yourself through using phrases that you find helpful can build resilience, help manage anxiety and impatience, and keep you going during challenging times.

For Itzel, the influencer from the previous chapter, her self-talk is filled with one phrase she finds extremely helpful, "Trust the process." This phrase helped Itzel overcome self-doubt when she first combined her passions by becoming a blogger and influencer. She used this self-talk to get through the beginning stages when she would ask herself "Are people going to care? Am I doing the right thing?"

Additionally, developing self-awareness of her self-talk has shaped her career and enabled her to think about her impact on others. When she noticed that her behavior and words had an impact on others, it motivated her to keep going. Through trusting the process, her influence was increasing—others were taking notice of the value she provided and thanking her for what she did for them.

If you're wondering how you can celebrate small wins related to your progress related to self-awareness, professional development or business growth, here's a step-by-step guide:

1. Take 5-10 minutes at least two times per week to identify the wins: Recognize even minor improvements or accomplishments in your self-awareness or professional growth.
2. Write it down: Record the win in a dedicated journal or digital note. Be specific about what you achieved.
3. Reflect on the process: Think about the steps you took to achieve this win. What worked well? What did you learn? What can you do more or less of?
4. Share with a supportive person: Tell a friend, family member, or mentor about your achievement and talk about why it's important to you.
5. Visualize the impact: Imagine how this small win contributes to your larger goals and professional growth journey.
6. Allow yourself to bask in the moment: Take a moment to let yourself feel and embrace the positive emotions associated with your accomplishment. What do you feel? How does it feel?
7. Treat yourself: Do something you enjoy as a small reward.
8. Express gratitude: Thank yourself for the effort you've put in, and if applicable, thank others who supported you.

9. Connect it to the bigger picture: Relate this small win to your larger professional or personal development goals.
10. Set a new micro-goal: Use the momentum from this win to set your next small, achievable target.
11. Review regularly: Set aside time weekly or monthly to look back at your collection of small wins.

Remember, the most important takeaway is to make celebration a habit. Consistently acknowledging your progress, no matter how small, can significantly boost motivation and reinforce positive behaviors in your self-awareness and professional development journey. And, when obstacles arise, you can look back on your list of wins to stay motivated.

How Did Shirley Turn It Around?

For Shirley, after ten years of building LUCA, she realized that she needed to make a change to find more balance. She implemented a succession plan so they could bring in an executive director to build and grow the organization. It was a very difficult decision because, oftentimes, founders can have a hard time taking a backseat.

"Having survived the pandemic, having survived that traumatic exit of key staff members in 2019, having felt personal stressors and challenges to my wellbeing both mental, physical, emotional, I knew that I had to take a break and that I had to do something that would allow me to have better balance. And so I shifted my role to serving on the board. I currently serve as a strategic growth officer, participating in strategic partnerships supporting the executive director and their role.

"My role as a board member gave me greater flexibility and more personal time. I was able to exercise four or five times a week and have dinner with my family. I could take vacations much more frequently and provide support to my parents who are elderly, and that felt good. I could still keep my heart and my hands in LUCA in other ways without being as hands-on.

"I felt that I was able to prioritize and do all of the things that are important to me personally, for the first time in a very long time. I think as women, too often we don't prioritize ourselves. Especially if you have children or a spouse or we get caught up working just to get through the grind of life. I found that it is important—and not a selfish or bad thing—to care as much for myself as others. It's not easy for me—I don't know if it's a Latina thing, where everybody else comes first. You serve everyone else before you sit down, which reminds me of my grandmother selflessly giving to me. But when you do that without feeding and fueling yourself, you will eventually be empty."

Today, both Shirley and LUCA are thriving. Serving as strategic growth officer allowed her the space she needed to focus on all that she cared about both personally and professionally. In early 2024, she made the decision to return to serve as executive director, stepping back into a more hands-on role with renewed energy and a sense of balance. LUCA continues to grow and increase the number of students they serve. Shirley's influence and leadership continue to expand through her work at LUCA; she is working on new ways to expand her nonprofit to have an even greater impact.

CHAPTER 7

INFLUENCE, LEVELED UP

"Failure is success if we learn from it."

MALCOLM FORBES

arla successfully turned her hobby into a profitable business but had to manage anxiety, self-doubt, and imposter syndrome along the way. Early on in her journey, she was highly aware of feeling anxious and had thoughts related to self-doubt (Square 1). At times, these inner obstacles prevented her from posting on social media or putting herself out there (Square 2). However, she decided she needed to do more to fully embrace her passion and purpose (Square 3). From playing back her own videos daily to celebrating small wins, Marla used various strategies (Square 4) to overcome her internal obstacles to affirm her message, build her confidence, build her brand, and keep pursuing her passion. Incorporating these strategies into her routine over time was the key to leveling up her influence.

As she progressed on her journey of turning her art into a business, she had ideas about expanding. Being a successful artist, selling art, doing what she loved, and giving back to her community was rewarding on multiple levels. However, managing her self-doubt, anxiety, and imposter syndrome through self-talk, celebrating wins, and playing back her own videos, she was able to realize a larger vision. Marla wanted to help other artists and business owners and she has broadened the scope of her work well beyond creating art.

One of Marla's current ventures is operating a multi-purpose art studio space. As an artist, she realized that while co-working spaces are a great business space solution for so many small businesses, these spaces were not made for artists. Using co-working spaces as a model, she has developed a unique space offering that can be used by anyone, but most importantly can be used by artists. She uses this space to teach art classes, offer corporate team-building events, and to host book signings and pop-ups. In line with her vision to help other artists, she is using her space to allow other artists to exhibit their work and host their own events to promote their art.

Another branch of Marla's level up is consulting with other artists on the business of art. After diving into the art world and getting to know a variety of artists, she learned firsthand about the concept of the "starving artist." Marla noticed that many artists lacked the business training to successfully turn their art into a thriving business. She now consults artists on how to market themselves and turn their art into a sustainable career.

Marla's longstanding vision to support small business owners and make people happy with her art has expanded well beyond promoting and frequenting local businesses and hanging her art in homes across the country. Combining these two, she is creating art for small businesses. Creating murals and paintings for businesses is creating an impact and bringing happiness on a larger scale.

Marla's advice to others on leveling up their influence includes a reminder that this applies to everyone—moms, influencers, business owners, leaders, artists. "Don't stay the same, get out of your comfort zone, take risks and bet on yourself."

Your Influence, Leveled Up

Understanding your inner obstacles, aligning with your values, and embracing your purpose unlocks your power to shape your behavior and the world around you. With this awareness, you can push past your comfort zone and level up your influence. In other words, your influence, leveled up, comes from increasing your self-awareness of your thoughts, feelings, values, and behaviors while *still* taking action toward your values and goals.

Practicing the 4-Square Model can build your self-awareness, allowing you to break free from being stuck and take action toward your goals. When you are aware of your actions toward your values and goals, it can build your confidence and maximize your ability to grow and influence others. Your influence, leveled up, happens when you expand your horizons further by exploring new opportunities and taking risks that align with your values and purpose.

Your influence, leveled up, is influencing and impacting different people in different ways. It's expanding on your work and purpose by branching out in new directions. It's being able to build on your success, take more calculated risks, and having the confidence to fail. Leveling up your influence is trusting the process and exploring new opportunities.

For Marla, her next level-up has expanded beyond creating happy art to helping other artists turn their art into thriving businesses. My next level-up has been increasing my influence and impact on the EDM DJ community and developing a very unique niche. Today, I'm working with people who've reached the top of their field, and they recognize that what's holding them back from taking the next step is their own self-awareness of their fears, doubts, and behaviors.

Your influence increases as you take more committed actions toward your goals. Although unhelpful thoughts and feelings are still present, you're less likely to allow them to get you stuck. And, the opposite of being stuck is psychological flexibility.

Psychological flexibility is the ability to adapt to life's challenges by recognizing your thoughts and behaviors and choosing to take action toward your values and goals. Developing psychological flexibility is the overarching purpose of ACT and an essential skill that effective leaders possess. By using the 4-Square Model as a guide, we can accept and acknowledge that difficult thoughts and feelings may show up and still *choose* values-based actions—thus, ultimately, making our potential for growth limitless.

4-Square Model for Psychological Flexibility

Using the 4-Square model increases your psychological flexibility, making it easier to navigate challenges and setbacks and take steps toward your goals. When you have psychological flexibility, you are better able to break free from limiting thoughts and feelings to pursue your goals. This flexibility allows you to have influence, leveled up because you are better able to identify solutions to problems, make sound decisions, and manage stress. Without being bogged down by difficult thoughts and feelings, you can focus more on pursuing your purpose.

Psychological flexibility allows you to become a better leader—your influence expands because you are authentic and consistent, and others can see that your actions are aligned with your values. Your goals reflect your values and long-term vision and you are not swayed from them by unhelpful thoughts and feelings. Your decision-making remains consistent and even-keeled, even during stressful situations. You can adapt to unexpected changes, navigate uncertainty, and stay focused on your long-term goals and vision no matter the circumstances.

Psychological flexibility helps you act toward your values and goals in new or challenging situations when anxiety and self-doubt are likely to show up. When Marla finds herself feeling anxious and doubting her ability to be a consultant, she reminds herself of her past accomplishments as well as her purpose and this enables her to continue taking steps to offer her knowledge to help other artists.

Similarly, when I question my own ability to help EDM DJs succeed in the music industry because I am not a DJ and I don't have experience on the business side of the industry, I remind myself of the value my knowledge as a psychologist has added to the careers of so many DJs. And, both Marla and I understand that growing causes discomfort, yet it can be very rewarding. When we fail, we still have an opportunity to learn.

Learning from failure develops resilience, the ability to bounce back after a crisis, another key benefit of psychological flexibility. Resilience allows you to maximize your growth and potential. You can keep going in the face of challenges and obstacles both personal and professional. You are committed to your goals and they remain in sync with what you care about and your why. Taking steps toward your goals help you to continually grow, even when you experience failure.

The more you develop psychological flexibility, the more you level up your influence. In addition to better decision-making when under stress, building resilience, and increased ability to stay true to your values, psychological flexibility promotes innovative thinking, improves emotional regulation, enhances problem-solving skills, and improves communication.

Psychological flexibility helps you manage your emotions during any situation while staying true to your values. When intense unhelpful emotions show up, you are able to take a step back and choose to act toward your values. Doing this can increase productivity because you spend less time feeling stuck. Not allowing emotions to take over also impacts those around you because others see you as even-keeled, authentic, consistent, and trustworthy. You become a role model and others look to you for guidance and advice.

The path to leveling up your influence begins with self-awareness as a stepping stone to growth. Using the 4-Square Model can help you break free from limiting thoughts and feelings and focus on taking action steps toward your goals. With the 4-Square Model as a compass to guide you, your potential for growth and as a leader is limitless.

Influence, Leveled Up: Caine's Story

Caine (DJ GT_Ofice) decided that he wanted to change careers and become a music producer and EDM DJ after a life-changing festival experience. He loved the music, the feeling it produced, and the culture of positivity. After working as an actor and in real estate, he discovered his purpose was music. However, he wasn't a trained musician, and he had no idea how he would make this dream of spreading positivity and happiness through his music a reality. Caine was determined, but the path forward would be filled with countless obstacles.

Putting out music for the first time, Caine experienced significant inner obstacles such as fear and self-doubt (Square 1). He was a new producer and he doubted himself. When he first released a track, he received a lot of negative feedback. The doubt became unbearable and he ended up taking the song down (Square 2)—an action he took in response to the fear and self-doubt.

Thankfully, he didn't stop producing. Instead, Caine learned from this experience and kept going. Caine cared about creating a legacy through his music and making people happy with his music (Square 3). Fear of rejection and criticism became a daily battle, but he loved what he was doing and he kept making music, taking steps toward his ultimate goal (Square 4). Having support from his family and friends kept him from giving up.

While working on his production skills, Caine got into radio, and, through his radio work, he connected with a mentor with decades of experience. His mentor would be the extra support he needed to level up.

Once he honed his production skills came the next obstacle—Caine felt it was taking forever to get a record deal. This led to feelings of disappointment and frustration. He knew his purpose was to release music to the world, but would it ever happen?

As the disappointment persisted, instead of getting stuck in unhelpful feelings of frustration and giving up on his dream, Caine focused more on what mattered—making music and finding a way to get it out into the world to bring others happiness. He started to wonder: If a record deal wasn't working out in the traditional way, what actions could he take toward his goals?

He came up with a solution: he would start his own record label. While he had no experience with starting or running a record label, he made the decision to figure it out. He embarked on something completely new—the business of running a record label. Fast forward to today, and Caine is running Caine Records and becoming a master in the business-side of running a label.

Self-doubt and worry are still a struggle, as is the stress of running a record label and wearing so many different hats when it comes to the business side, producing, and being a DJ. Having to continually face criticism when a song doesn't do as well as he hoped is still a challenge. But what keeps Caine going is knowing that people love the music and that he's part of the EDM community, which he loves. Another strategy that helps Caine continue on this difficult path is thinking about when he's gone, the legacy he will leave behind through his music. "It's an emotional rollercoaster of highs and lows in this industry. I'm not where I want to be yet but I also realize that others would love to be where I am. Keeping this in perspective also helps."

Through support from family, friends, mentors, and fans, Caine has been able to reach some of his goals. To date, he has released several songs that topped the Billboard charts through Caine Records. He continues to make more music and run the label and is considering multiple ways to expand his business beyond releasing music to help up-and-coming artists navigate the challenges he has faced as a new producer and DJ in the EDM world.

Influence, Leveled Up: My Story

I made a successful career as a psychology-based, executive coach working with leaders across a variety of industries. In parallel, due to my growing love of EDM festivals and music, I got to know the DJ community and realized they were experiencing a lot of the same level-up issues that I'd seen in my executive coaching.

For years, inner obstacles such as thinking I couldn't do it and that it wasn't possible to start the career that mattered to me (Square 1) prevented me from setting new goals. It felt impossible; I continued my clinical job and avoided exploring ways to fulfill my professional dreams in a new direction (Square 2). What was important to me professionally was helping leaders be more successful and making workplaces better. And what was important to me personally was EDM music and the EDM community (Square 3).

Learning about the power of ACT and implementing the 4-Square Model was the key to unlocking my inner leader and taking a huge risk that aligned with my values to make a career shift. Using the 4-Square model, I've learned to label and accept the many inner obstacles that have come up for me while making a career shift. Along with this acceptance, I got clear on my values and purpose, and worked with a coach to develop an action plan for starting my consulting practice (Square 4). Along the way, I combined my passion for helping business leaders be more successful with my passion for EDM music and the EDM community.

Today, I've made it my mission to help as many DJs to level up as I can. I do this through social media, this book, consulting, and customized coaching programs with the many DJs I now serve. While I still have anxieties, doubts, and fears daily, I'm able to stay focused on my mission and take daily steps toward my goal. I notice my thoughts related to self-doubt and anxiety, but I don't let them sway me from my goal.

Like Marla, I focus on celebrating all progress and small wins. Like Therese, I connect with like-minded colleagues and mentors for support. Like Itzel, I talk myself through the challenging times and remind myself that "In the middle of difficulty lies opportunity." And, I work with an executive coach who helps me build my business skills and address the challenges that come with branching out into the unknown.

The process of developing services and products to help DJs reach their goals at every career level has been filled with research, trial and error. However, I recognize that I'm still learning and keep my mission and purpose at the forefront while I keep going. The positive feedback I receive from countless DJs also keeps me motivated. While delivering my current offerings to DJs, I'm also considering larger ideas to partner and collaborate with others to help further expand my mission of reaching more DJs to help them overcome obstacles holding them back and level up.

The biggest piece in leveling up my influence has been my self-awareness of unhelpful thoughts and feelings; learning to allow and accept thoughts such as "I can't _____", "I don't know enough", and "I won't be good at _____" without letting those thoughts stop me. I am confident in who and what is important and I know my *why*. Knowing how to handle unhelpful thoughts has been freeing; I've been able to take action, successfully serving a new niche and helping EDM DJs reach their goals. I know that with risk comes the potential for failure and that failure can be the best way to learn and grow.

When you become aware of your inner obstacles, and can accept fear and self-doubt and not allow them to get you stuck, then you can choose to take action toward your purpose and values, moving you toward your goals. Self-awareness of what gets you stuck and what your values and purpose are is what guides you to achieve growth that would otherwise not be possible. By building psychological flexibility, you are better primed to make sound decisions, solve problems, and influence others. As our stories show, such increased flexibility not only increases your influence but also allows you to expand your thinking and reach the next level in your career or business.

> **Self-awareness of what gets you stuck and what your values and purpose are is what guides you to achieve growth that would otherwise not be possible.**

The 4-square model is your guide to identifying your inner obstacles and accepting them while simultaneously being aware of your values and purpose and actively taking steps toward them. You can complete the 4-square model for your professional or personal obstacles and goals and you can also apply the 4-square model to specific situations where inner obstacles may show up and get in your way. Here's a quick review of the model:

The 4 squares of the ACT matrix include your internal world (thoughts, feelings, values) and your behaviors that others can see. The bottom two squares describe your inner world which includes what you care about, and unhelpful thoughts and feelings you experience. The top two squares represent your actions or behaviors and are the things you do in response to your inner experience. The squares on the left side of the page comprise your unhelpful thoughts and feelings (bottom left square) and what you do when you get hooked or stuck from these thoughts and feelings (top left square). The squares on the right side of the page include your values and who and what is important to you (bottom right square) and what you do when you are acting toward your values (top right square).

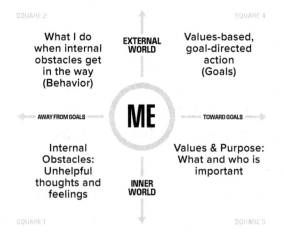

Level Up Your Influence: Awareness Assessment

I hope you've enjoyed this self-awareness guide to maximizing your growth and unlocking your inner leader. To close out the book, let's take a look at your current level of self-awareness as it relates to the 4-square model, and identify where you are with working toward your goals and breaking free from your inner obstacles.

Answer each question using the following rating scale:

1 | Rarely/Not at all
2 | Sometimes/Somewhat
3 | Often/Mostly
4 | Very often/Very clear
5 | Always/Extremely clear

1. How often do you notice unhelpful thoughts or feelings arising during your day-to-day activities?
2. When you experience challenging emotions or thoughts, how do you typically respond to them?
3. Can you identify any recurring patterns of behavior that you engage in when faced with inner obstacles?
4. To what extent are you able to accept and work with your inner obstacles, rather than trying to eliminate them entirely?
5. How clear are you about your core personal values? Can you easily list your top 3-5 values?

6. In what ways do your daily actions and decisions align with or conflict with your stated values?

7. How would you describe your sense of purpose or mission in life? How confident are you in this description?

8. What specific goals have you set that relate to your values and purpose?

9. What concrete action steps are you currently taking to move toward these goals?

10. How open are you to exploring and potentially changing your thoughts, feelings, and behaviors in pursuit of professional and personal growth?

Scoring: Add your scores from all questions to determine your level of self-awareness.

Total Score Ranges:

- ➔ **10-25: Beginning Awareness**
- ➔ **26-40: Developing Awareness**
- ➔ **41-50: Advanced Awareness**

Steps for each range:

Beginning Awareness (10-25):
1. Start a daily mindfulness practice (3-5 minutes) to increase self-awareness.
2. Begin a daily journaling habit to explore your thoughts, feelings, and behaviors.
3. Read self-help books on personal growth and emotional intelligence.

Developing Awareness (26-40):
1. Expand your mindfulness practice to 10-20 minutes daily.
2. Engage in regular self-reflection exercises to deepen your understanding of your values and purpose.
3. Set small, achievable goals aligned with your values and track your progress.
4. Seek feedback from trusted friends or colleagues about your behaviors and blind spots.

Advanced Awareness (41-50):
1. Maintain your current mindfulness and self-reflection practices.
2. Challenge yourself to set more ambitious goals aligned with your purpose.
3. Continue learning professional growth techniques and strategies from other like-minded professionals.

This scoring system provides a general framework for self-assessment. Remember that self-awareness is a continual journey, and at every stage, even though you may score within the "Advanced Awareness" category, you can still benefit from ongoing reflection and growth. And, here's how coaching can help you achieve your goals faster at any level. If you scored in the "Beginning Awareness" range, you might benefit most from professional guidance in developing your self-awareness and personal growth strategies. If you scored in the "Developing Awareness" range, working with a coach can help you accelerate your professional growth, overcome plateaus, and gain new perspectives on your professional development journey. If you scored in the "Advanced Awareness" range, working with a coach can help you push your boundaries and achieve even higher levels of professional growth.

As you move forward on your path to growth, here are a few guiding questions to think about:

- ➜ What does it mean to you to 'level up'?
- ➜ What might your 'level up' look like?
- ➜ What words, phrases and actions come to mind?
- ➜ Which of these are internal just to you?
- ➜ Which of these are external, and occur as you interact with others?
- ➜ What actions can you take on your path to leveling up?

ACKNOWLEDGMENTS

First, I would like to thank my mom for her ongoing support and encouragement throughout this process.

To my friends and colleagues, who have been my cheerleaders, sounding boards, and source of strength throughout this process, your support has made this book possible, and I am grateful for each of you. Thank you, Joy, for acting as an extra pair of eyes and helping me meet deadlines.

To Eland Robert Mann, my editor, your insight and guidance not only exponentially improved this book but also made the writing journey far less solitary and much more rewarding.

Thank you to my beta readers, Kulliki Keller, Christian Lampasso, and Marc Sokol, who each provided invaluable feedback and thoughtful suggestions to improve the content and flow of this book. Kulliki, as an expert in ACT, your input was essential. Christian, as an expert in business and marketing, your attention to detail and suggestions to make it more reader-friendly were extremely valuable. Marc,

I appreciate your ongoing guidance, support, and suggestions on the book and in my career as a consultant.

To Dana Gionta, my writing accountability partner, your support helped me to stay motivated and get this book done.

To each of the interviewees – Therese Mascardo, Robert Cioffi, Shirley Acavedo-Buontempo, Caine Sheppard, Marla Beth Enowitz, and Itzel Auguilera, I appreciate your vulnerability in sharing your challenges and successes on your professional journeys.

To Mira Brancu, as a mentor and author, you have inspired me and helped me be more strategic with my business, and especially with my writing. You've also motivated me to try new things and have been an ongoing source of support.

To Marla, in addition to being an interviewee, thank you for providing the inspiration for the cover art and colors. George B. Stevens, thank you for bringing our vision for the cover to life and making it even better than I could have imagined.

ABOUT THE AUTHOR

Dr. Sunni Lampasso is a coaching psychologist, consultant, DJ advisor, and speaker, who has enabled countless leaders to unlock their potential through psychology-based coaching strategies. Leveraging two decades of experience as a clinician, she helps individuals from a wide variety of industries develop their inner leader and maximize professional growth.

While her background lies in elevating C-suite executives and driving business results, Sunni has carved an unexpected niche in the dynamic world of electronic dance music. Recognizing striking parallels between the challenges of CEOs and EDM artists, she now guides DJs and music professionals in areas like peak performance mindset, authentic personal branding, and sustainable career strategies including wellness. By fusing her psychological expertise with a profound passion for the dance music community, Sunni is catalyzing transformative growth for a new breed of industry trailblazers.

More from Sunni

Email: Sunni@shapingsuccessconsulting.com
Instagram: @shaping_success
LinkedIn: https://www.linkedin.com/in/sunnilampasso/
Website: https://www.shapingsuccessconsulting.com/

Printed in the USA
CPSIA information can be obtained
at www.ICGtesting.com
LVHW022054221024
794540LV00003B/4